STARTING
WITH THE
PEOPLE

BOOKS BY DANIEL YANKELOVICH

Ego and Instinct:
The Psychoanalytic View
of Human Nature — Revised
(coauthor)

The Changing Values on Campus:
Political and Personal Attitudes of
Today's College Students

The New Morality:
A Profile of American Youth in the 1970s

Work, Productivity, and Job Satisfaction
(coauthor)

New Rules:
Searching for Self-Fulfillment
in a World Turned Upside Down

The World at Work:
An International Report on Jobs,
Productivity, and Human Values
(coauthor)

STARTING
WITH THE
PEOPLE

*Daniel Yankelovich and
Sidney Harman*

HOUGHTON MIFFLIN COMPANY

Boston

1988

Library of Congress Cataloging-in-Publication Data

Yankelovich, Daniel.
Starting with the people.
Bibliography: p.
Includes index.
1. United States—Military policy—Public opinion.
2. United States—Economic policy—Public opinion—
1981–   . 3. Public opinion—United States.
I. Harman, Sidney, date. II. Title.
UA23.Y25   1988   355'.0335'73   88-875
ISBN 0-395-47695-X

Printed in the United States of America

Q 10 9 8 7 6 5 4 3 2 1

Charts designed by Ronn Campisi.

Acknowledgments

This book grew out of a project that began in 1981. Daniel Yankelovich and Congressman Les Aspin formed the New Framework Group, which Sidney Harman joined shortly thereafter. The purpose of the New Framework Group was to explore the implications of our shared conviction that sweeping cultural and political changes have made the liberalism and conservatism of the past obsolete, and that new political frameworks are needed. The list of those who participated in the group's discussions and who made important contributions to the thinking reflected in this book is a long one. It starts first and foremost with Les Aspin, who has thought deeply about the issues raised here and has helped to shape this work's main thesis.

A number of people have given us invaluable help and guidance—in particular, Hassie Yankelovich and Jane Harman, and also Shirley Hufstedler, Bernard Schwartz, Isabel Sawhill, Amitai Etzioni, David Cohen, Jack Sparks, James Chace, Richard Smoke, Leon Shapiro, Robert Kingston, Gar

Alperovitz, C. Fred Bergsten, John Gardner, Peter Brown, Ted Ashley, Ira Magaziner, Ruben Mettler, Alan Kay, Randall Forsberg, Robert Hodes, T. George Harris, Robert Nathan, Norman Ornstein, Michael Pertschuk, Alice Rivlin, Peter Szanton, Florence Skelly, and Arthur White.

We also wish to thank David Matthews, Ernest Boyer, Irving Bluestone, Peter Edelman, Clark Kerr, Joel Perwin, John Diebold, Edmund Brown, Jr., Mark Uhlig, Lisle Carter, Lawrence Cremin, Madelyn Hochstein, Larry Kaagan, William Eastham, Murray Finley, Pierson Grieve, Keith Keener, Maurice Lazarus, Michael Maccoby, Roger Mollander, Thomas Graham, William Ruder, John Sawhill, and Lester Thurow.

Mary Komarnicki gave invaluable help with analysis of the data, preparation of the charts, and attention to the details of final preparation. Her contribution has been a significant one.

We also wish to acknowledge the research contributions of Randall Rothenberg, Tania Melich, Matthew Greenwald, Deborah Barron, and Adam Stagliano. The staff of the Roper Center's data base (POLL) is due a special note of appreciation.

Sona Beshar prepared the manuscript for production with great skill and patience, as did Mary McCleary. Michael Janeway and Liz Duvall at Houghton Mifflin provided important guidance and adept editing of the text. Thanks also to Ronn Campisi and Walter Komarnicki for their professionalism in designing the charts.

JOHN IMMERWAHR

The authors are deeply indebted to John Immerwahr, who collaborated with us in developing this book from its first conception. He contributed significantly to the research, analysis, and writing at virtually every stage of the process. Immerwahr is a professor of philosophy at Villanova University.

Contents

Foreword

BY CYRUS VANCE

THERE IS A MAXIM in business circles that behind every problem lurks a hidden opportunity. All Americans today hope this saying is true, for our nation is surely beset with problems. I believe there *are* significant opportunities lurking behind the problems Daniel Yankelovich and Sidney Harman confront in this excellent and timely book.

The authors are concerned with two facets of the new competitive challenges to our nation—from the Soviet Union on the military and ideological side, and from Japan and others on the economic side. They are particularly concerned that the values of the American people help to shape the policies that are developed in the future to meet these challenges.

I share their convictions. I have long believed that without the understanding and broad support of our citizens, we cannot have effective foreign and domestic policies. I am also convinced that such support must be rooted in public values embraced by a majority of our citizens.

Adapting to change, whether it involves the individual or

the nation, is difficult and often painful. As the authors point out, our nation is beginning to experience the discomfort. We must therefore make sure that we also take advantage of the potential benefits of the broad changes, economic and political, that are taking place.

In the international arena, the Soviet Union presents us with a novel and difficult problem. Under Secretary-General Gorbachev, the Soviet leadership has been forced to recognize that the "correlation of forces" is running against the USSR. The secretary-general has made it clear that the Soviet Union cannot hope to revitalize its stagnant economy and address the other pressing domestic problems it faces unless it provides greater openness for its people and achieves a radical restructuring of its economy involving a huge reallocation of resources. These daunting objectives cannot be realized without a breathing spell in external affairs, which will permit the Soviet Union to concentrate on its domestic problems. These circumstances present the American people with an opportunity to strengthen our national security and at the same time relieve the strain on our own economy. This is an opportunity we have not seen for many years.

Here at home, our economy is also causing us to re-examine the fundamentals. After years of eroding leadership in technology, innovation, and product quality in the manufacturing sector, the American economy is facing the new realities of international competition, and progress in technology is spurting ahead even more rapidly than in the past. These and other changes may be creating dislocations, but they too present new opportunities to improve the American standard of living, provided that we bring the requisite political will and wisdom to bear.

Many of our nation's best thinkers are engaged in examining the implications of these changes for America's future. The authors of *Starting with the People* add a unique perspective to this examination. They are convinced that to take advantage of the opportunities that change is creating, average Americans must play a crucial role. But this is not easy to accomplish, because some of the issues are so mired in technical complexity that they have become largely the province of the experts. This is especially true in the areas of national security and economic policy, where for many years experts have dominated. The question posed then is, how, under these circumstances, can average citizens play a proper and decisive role in shaping the nation's destiny? The authors confront this issue head-on—with results that are enlightening and often startling.

As secretary of state and as a lawyer involved in business matters for more than thirty-five years, I have been convinced of the importance of the public in creating and sustaining successful national policies. Many political leaders insist that "the public matters—the public counts." But in practice they ignore the public. Because foreign and economic policies are typically formulated by a handful of government officials after discussion among themselves and their experts, these are matters about which the public typically knows and hears too little. Yet, as I learned from my time in the Defense Department and the State Department, the support of the public is critical if our policies are to succeed and endure.

In short, a bridge must be built between the theoretical acknowledgment that the public is important and the development of real live consensus in support of new policies. We have learned from hard experience that in the absence of public understanding and support, our leaders too often embark upon policies only to discover later that they are blocked because Congress and the public do not support them.

The policy process has two aspects—one visible, the other invisible. Actions taken by a policy maker who is confident of the facts, confident of the expert analysis of his or her judgment, is the visible part. When, however, the policy maker fails to take public values into account, he or she may well find the chosen policy blocked or frustrated by the invisible aspect of the process.

A case in point from my own experience is the successful resolution of the long-festering Panama Canal problem in the first year of the Carter administration. When we came to office, it was clear to the president and his advisers that resolving this thorny problem was necessary to protect our national interests by ensuring unimpeded operation of the canal for the foreseeable future. At the time, there was little question in my mind that if we failed to resolve this issue, Panama would sooner or later resort to violence, even to the point of destroying the canal. I shared with President Carter the conviction that the prompt conclusion of a fair treaty with Panama would serve our interests and the cause of peace and security in the region.

We recognized, however, that the negotiation of a new treaty carried with it serious political risks. National opinion polls showed that Americans were nine to one against negotiating a new treaty. This overwhelmingly negative attitude was reflected in the views of many members of Congress. We decided to embark on a campaign of public debate and discussion that would present to the electorate all of the alternative choices, pro and con. We had faith that once people gave real thought to the issue, they would recognize the desirability of moving forward and would in the end support a new treaty. After an intense public debate, the majority did come to support the treaty, which was adopted and ratified by both nations.

Another area in which public support is essential is arms control. In the future, public debate will be needed to resolve issues of mutual, or common, security. While serving as a member of the Independent Commission on Disarmament and Security Issues, I endorsed the commission's recommendation that in today's nuclear world, the concept of common or mutual security is the correct and realistic basis for sound national security policy vis-à-vis the Soviet Union. At that time I wrote, "In short, the most basic security for the superpowers—security from nuclear war—cannot in the final analysis be dominated by competition. Their security must be based on an unparalleled degree of cooperation. It must be common security." As yet, the public and the political leaders have not come together on this issue. *Starting with the People* addresses this question and shows the conditions under which both our leaders and the American people would accept it. I find the authors' analysis persuasive.

On the economic side, as the authors point out, we have permitted serious erosion of our economic competitiveness. I have long believed that we must rebuild and modernize our economic base in order to achieve sustained economic growth, and that we have contributed to our competitive problems by living off our economic capital, permitting plants and equipment to deteriorate as we shifted to a service economy. This corrosive trend has been exacerbated by the short time horizon of many sectors of the financial community. The second part of *Starting with the People* contains a cogent discussion of these issues, along with proposals for solutions rooted in public values.

Daniel Yankelovich and Sidney Harman have excellent credentials. One has long been at the forefront of scholarly and practical work on interpreting the public mind, the other in the vanguard of hands-on management and entrepreneurial activity. The conclusions they reach and the recommendations they offer flow from broad personal experience.

This book is important because it provides a realistic

guide for interpreting the meaning of change. It combines wise theory with hard practical conclusions. Policy makers and public alike will find it thought-provoking and illuminating.

STARTING
WITH THE
PEOPLE

Introduction

WHEN HISTORIANS LOOK BACK at the Reagan presidency, they will find an old-fashioned morality tale. Ronald Reagan was not the first president to win election by appealing to the values of the American people. But he was the most skillful at presenting himself as the embodiment of the traditional American creed: patriotism, family, self-reliance, principle above expediency.

"Private values," said President Reagan in his 1986 state-of-the-union message, "must be at the heart of public policy." Intuitively, Mr. Reagan understood that important issues always revolve around questions of values. His emphasis on such themes was the key to his electoral successes. In both of his winning campaigns, in 1980 and 1984, he managed to shift the electoral battleground from a politics of issues to a politics of values. By accusing the welfare state of subverting the principles Americans most cherish, Mr. Reagan stirred voter resentment against political liberalism on the domestic front. On the international scene, he blamed liberals for turning the country into a loser, and he persuaded voters that President Carter's policies had frustrated their hopes for America by undermining American exceptionalism—the belief that the United States is a nation set apart, special.

During his first six years in office, Mr. Reagan was one of the most highly esteemed presidents in American history. The deepest source of his popularity, as revealed in studies of public attitudes, was neither his personality nor his skill as a communicator; it was the public's perception of him as a man who stood up for his principles and who was tough enough not to fold under pressure. For six years this image was untarnished. However, once the American people learned that Mr. Reagan, contrary to his ideals, did in fact swap arms for hostages, public confidence in the president fell more precipitously *than at any time in the history of opinion polling.*[1] The reason: he had betrayed both his stated values and the public's deeply held ones. The key principle he was seen to violate was America's honor in yielding to blackmail. The public view was that under no circumstances should we knuckle under to Ayatollah Khomeini, however terrible the consequences—even the death of the hostages. That lapse into moral blindness eroded much of Ronald Reagan's credibility.

Our book is about the public's values and about policies that are blind to them. That blindness is a grave fault in a brutally competitive world. It leads to vacillation and mixed signals to our friends and opponents, and at its worst it threatens to undermine both America's standard of living and its national security. We believe that one of the keys to future peace and prosperity is to match the nation's policies to the values of the people. The purpose of the book is to suggest how this goal might be met.

Over the past fifteen years new forms of competitiveness among nations have been on the rise, and our national consensus about how to cope with these realities has vanished. Global competitiveness has come from Japan and other aggressive trading nations in the economic sphere and from the Soviet Union on military and political fronts. In the face of these threats, the nation's leaders are divided; the public is also divided, and the public and the leaders are in turn divided from each other. The leaders are polarized along ideological lines. The public is volatile and anxious. Our political leaders are unable to define a long-term strategy for the country that the public will steadfastly support.

For many years after World War II America was able to manage its involvement with the rest of the world surefootedly and responsibly, because the country's political leaders, Republican and Democratic alike, enjoyed the support of a firm national consensus. Unswervingly, the public supported America's Cold War struggle with the Soviet Union, the building of alliances within the United Nations and all over the world, the expansion of worldwide free trade, and the policy of reconciliation with, and to, our principal World War II enemies, Germany and Japan.

Then, in the 1970s, the consensus collapsed. The war in Vietnam was one of the causes; there were others. Since that time the nation has floundered. But the decisions America faces require a new consensus.

Competitiveness from abroad is, in at least one respect, novel. It is familiar in that it concerns front-page subjects — the nuclear arms race, the U.S. trade deficit, wars in other parts of the globe, terrorism and anti-Americanism, oil cartels, Third World demands for a larger piece of the economic pie, competition with the Soviets for political influence in the Third World, competition with the Japanese for dominance in global markets. It raises a specter most Americans don't think about very much: other nations are growing increasingly uncomfortable with this country's dominant position.

Most Americans are unaware of the impact their country has on other nations and cultures. We Americans find it disquieting to realize that large numbers in the Muslim world, for example, hate and fear the very values that from our perspective make life worth living.

The conviction runs deep that our values are the best in the world: nine out of ten Americans believe the "American way of life is superior to that of any other country,"[2] and most Americans (81 percent) also believe that "the United States has a special role to play in the world today," which is different from the role of any other nation.[3] This theme of American exceptionalism — the belief that the United States is uniquely destined by God to effect good in the world — was strong at the birth of the nation. It remains strong today. Americans take it for granted that since our values are the best in the world and our mission is blessed by God, American power is benign and will be seen as such by all except our enemies. In fact, however, the growth of American power has provoked in many countries a great fear and a determination to assert their own will.

This is not an unreasonable reaction. When a nation's power grows to a point where it affects the destinies of others (even if the powerful one is unaware of its impact), a backlash is inevitable. All over the world, other countries have targeted the United States as their principal opponent or competitor, and they are bringing immense vitality — and considerable success — to their challenges.

The well-being of the United States demands that Americans reach consensus on how to respond, especially with respect to arms and the economy.

In the case of arms, how important is it for America to regain military superiority? How should America balance the threat posed by the nuclear arms race with the threat of

Soviet expansionism? How do we really feel about the ideological struggle with Soviet communism? Is America, as some believe, engaged in a struggle to the death with the Soviets, in which one side or the other must eventually prevail? Or can we seek and find a "live and let live" accommodation?

In the case of the economy, what sacrifices are Americans prepared to make to compete more vigorously against Japanese products and services in world markets? How far is America prepared to travel down the protectionist road? How active do Americans want their government to be in order to revitalize competitiveness? How strong is the national will to compete? Is it strong enough to motivate Americans to improve the quality of their products? To induce management to abandon its obsession with short-term profits? To inspire management and labor to work together against the external threat? To persuade our schools and colleges to improve the quality of American education?

By the early 1990s, Americans need to come together on these questions, much as they developed a common view about how to deal with Germany, Japan, and the Soviet Union in the postwar era. All voters need not think alike: a general attitude shared by two thirds will suffice for a working consensus. If the nation is of one mind about how to meet these challenges from abroad, the chances for effective action are excellent. But if there is no shared outlook, the United States will drift. It will lurch indecisively from one faction's policy to another. And it will continue to flounder, as it has for more than a decade.

The nation's leaders and experts are well aware of the need to create a consensus. They know how frustrating it is for the country to function without one. But sad to say, though they are proficient in their own fields, most experts are naive about creating a national consensus. It is an enigma to them. Worse yet, they are oblivious of the extent to which they themselves contribute to the problem.

The conventional strategy for seeking consensus is for experts first to define the issues and then to attempt to "educate" the public. An army of professional communicators, in advertising, public relations, lobbying, and the media, package and promote ideas in the effort to acquaint the public with the leaders' thinking and to engineer the consent of the governed. In this model, the experts operate on the premise that they alone possess the necessary knowledge to shape the policies on which they seek consensus. They assume that the public, in its ignorance of the issues, has little of value to contribute to formulating policies. Lacking essential information, the public needs to be educated so that it can better understand and support the experts' conclusions.

When experts talk about creating consensus and communicating with the public, they have in mind this familiar concept. In theory they may give lip service to dialogue with the public, but in practice communication is strictly one-directional. Many experts are good at talking to the public. But when it comes to *listening*, liberals and conservatives alike have a tin ear — a deaf spot that distances them from what the average voter is trying to tell them.

If this strategy of one-way communication worked well, consensus building would be simply a matter of giving more information to the electorate. But the strategy is so badly flawed that if the amount of information conveyed to the public were doubled or quadrupled, the result would be not more consensus but even greater divisiveness and polarization.

Our conclusion, based on many years of analysis of public opinion, is that the American people have grown profoundly resistant to this type of communication. The public may give the impression of going along, but the impression is misleading. Invisible layers of public resistance to expertise manifest themselves, undermining the best efforts of policy makers. On matters such as the Strategic Defense Initiative (SDI) or trade policy, public support mysteriously vanishes just when officials are sure the electorate is with them. The frustration of this experience leaves our leaders with the conviction that people are ignorant and fickle, and that they must therefore learn to manipulate the public more skillfully, or even to bypass it altogether.

Why the resistance to expert-defined solutions? Its main source is the public's demand for a larger role in shaping life-and-death policies. People do not buy the premise that their role is merely to listen passively, absorb the information the experts dish out, and then choose among contending options, all of them defined by experts. In foreign policy especially there has been a steady democratization during the past few decades as, in the aftermath of the war in Vietnam, the public has insisted on having a greater say.

The experts' deaf ear to the public was no obstacle when elites had a monopoly on foreign policy decisions. That is no longer the case. The experts' presumption that they alone have the answers now collides head-on with the public's clamor for a larger role.

Creating a national consensus in the 1990s, though difficult, is no more daunting than many other tasks the nation has successfully accomplished. The key is a proper understanding of the cause of the absence of consensus during the past decade and a half. It is surprisingly simple: the cause is a fallacy that pervades American life and culture and that is easy to grasp in the abstract, though hard to deal with concretely.

This fallacy is the generally accepted belief that policy decisions on important issues such as the nuclear arms race and the trade deficit are *information-driven,* whereas in reality they are *value-driven.* If we believe that information is the key resource for making decisions, then the best-qualified decision makers are those with the most information — the experts. But if the heart and soul of decision making is a matter of values, then those who possess specialized information have no monopoly.

The relationship of information and values to decisions is a complex one. Information must of course be *part* of the process, but as we shall see, it plays a secondary role — in the literal sense, that it comes second. What comes first is the individual's stance on values. The public uses information to learn how to apply its values. But the values, not the information, are the primary determinants.

It should be kept in mind that experts, in arriving at their own judgments, rely on values just as much as the public does. They seem more dependent on information because they mask their personal values with technical language. But policy makers, like the rest of us, are inevitable prisoners of their subcultures. One cause of Detroit's delay in responding to the invasion of small Japanese and German cars in the 1960s was the anti–small-car bias of the American automotive culture. The barons of the industry were in love with big cars, and they convinced themselves that American consumers would never take to small, economical automobiles. This conviction reflected a value of their subculture and was held stubbornly in the face of masses of market research information that contradicted it.

Once we accept the premise that values come before information, for experts as well as for the public, the requirements for consensus building begin to fall into place. The most important one is that values must be brought into the open, so that conflicts between competing values can be resolved.

When values conflict, as they often do, it is difficult for the public to reach consensus. Americans typically want to cut down on government spending but preserve costly social programs. They want to cut farm subsidies but save the small farmer. They want to crack down on crime by throwing more felons in jail, but they don't want to build more prisons (especially near their neighborhoods). This is the familiar stuff of everyday political life in America. The penalty for failing to resolve conflicting values is public inconstancy. And no consensus is possible as long as public opinion remains volatile; a consensus cannot be built on shifting sands.

Significantly, public opinion polls show that on some issues, the people's positions are rocklike in their constancy. An example is public attitudes toward capital punishment. Firm public support for capital punishment has not wavered by more than two or three percentage points over a fifteen- to twenty-year period. On other issues, however — especially the ones that concern us here — public attitudes are still in a state of flux.

When is opinion firm and when is it unstable? It is firm when the public has resolved its conflicting values. It is unstable when the process of reaching a value judgment is blocked, or frustrated, or simply has not run its course.

In this book we distinguish between "mass opinion" and "public judgment." "Mass opinion" refers to the volatile, confused, ill-formed, and emotionally clouded public responses to an issue when underlying value conflicts remain unresolved. "Public judgment" refers to the public's viewpoint once people have had an opportunity to confront an issue for an extended period of time and to arrive at a settled conviction. It represents people's second thoughts after they have pondered an issue deeply enough to resolve all conflicts and tradeoffs and to accept responsibility for the consequences of their beliefs. Converting mass opinion into public judgment is no easy task. It can take months or years or even decades to accomplish.

To form a consensus on the two most fateful policy issues for the United States today, arms and the economy, the public must wrestle with some difficult questions of values — how fiercely to oppose communism as an ideology, what weight to give to the threat of nuclear war, how much to sacrifice to regain U.S. competitiveness against the Japanese, and so forth. Reaching judgment through a resolution of clashes of values is hard work, especially if sacrifices are needed. If trusted leaders deny the need for choices and tell the American people that they can have it all — a defense buildup *and* reduced taxes *and* a balanced budget — then people will avoid reality until they are obliged to face it. The result is a failure to resolve inherent value conflicts.

We believe the way to create a dialogue that will lead to a new national consensus is to recognize the significance of values and focus on finding policies that fit public values. The first step is to restate existing policy choices by wresting them out of the framework of technical expertise and putting them into a framework of public values. Consider the nuclear arms race. The policy of nuclear deterrence is the creation of technical experts in the arms control and foreign policy community. For more than forty years America and the Soviet Union have entangled themselves in a policy of mutual insecurity, deterring each other through the threat of "mutual assured destruction." This policy has remained opaque to the public, who nonetheless suspect that in the long run, a nuclear balance of terror must eventually break down, with cataclysmic consequences. Despite this threat, the experts continue to embrace nuclear deterrence. Although the two superpowers have recently made progress toward reducing the less dangerous, short-range portion of their arsenals, their long-range strategic nuclear arsenals remain over-stocked, and on this score there has been little progress in halting the nuclear arms race.

In Part I of this book we examine U.S.-Soviet relations and the arms race from the point of view of public values rather than from the perspective of arms control experts. In this light a host of new possibilities present themselves.

In Part II we turn from military and political competition to economic competition. Starting with public values, we find striking similarities between the two forms, and once again an opportunity to escape a dangerous impasse.

The problem in this case is the nation's failure to reverse a pattern of flagging American competitiveness against Japan and other countries. Here also American policy has been the brainchild of technical experts. Economic decision making is concentrated among a tiny group of people — bankers, economists, government officials, arbitrageurs, takeover lawyers, junk-bond specialists. These are the big-time players in the U.S. economy today. They make the spectacular economic decisions, ranging from leveraged buyouts of giant corporations to regulation of the money supply. The public is effectively excluded.

In boxing circles there is an old saying that you can't beat someone with no one. As long as the only policies people know of are the expert ones, they may grumble in dissatisfaction, but they have no way of knowing what they really want. The key to moving from volatile mass opinion to stable public judgment, and then to consensus, is to formulate policies known to be consistent with the public's own values.

In each of the two parts of this book we carry out a search for policies that match the public's values. With respect to U.S.-Soviet relations, our search leads to what we call a policy of "common security" — a blend of competition and cooperation with the Soviets that fits the realities of the nuclear age as well as America's basic values. With respect to trade competition, our analysis of public values and economic realities leads to a policy we call "more for more." It is predicated on the judgment that the country is ready (under proper conditions) to stimulate a great burst of economic energy, and that the individual jobholder holds the key to strengthening U.S. competitiveness. The nation's human resources are the only large-scale underutilized wellspring of advantage left to America, for other countries match us now in capital, technology, production efficiency, cost controls, and marketing.

At first glance, the idea of starting with the public's values to deal with issues about which an immense store of specialized knowledge must be acquired may seem to carry populism to an untenable extreme. But in practice this approach does not negate the legitimate place of expertise or wreak simplistic havoc on that which is complex. We are not denying the importance of expert knowledge; we are inverting its priority in relation to public values. Instead of asking, "How can the experts' recommendations be sold to the voters?" our approach starts with the public's values and asks whether there are sound policies that can match them.

Our thesis is that the nuclear arms race and the trade deficit are not really technical problems like the AIDS plague or toxic waste disposal, which will yield only to expert solutions. When reframed in a larger context, the issues of global competitiveness reveal themselves at the core as matters of values, convictions, goals, and priorities. They are political issues, best resolved through an approach that the philosopher Hannah Arendt called "representative thinking," which she rightfully regarded as the heart of the democratic political process. On matters where public judgment depends on values rather than on scientific inquiry, the best path is to bring the collective wisdom to bear by examining each issue from as many different aspects as possible.

It is the central thesis of this book that dynamic policies for dealing with these two awesome issues of our time — competition with the Soviets and competition with the Japanese and others — can be found in the political will of the many rather than in the technical cleverness of the few. If this is true, then the only sensible way to approach the issues is to start with the people.

I

Competing with the Soviets

1

Van Winkle's Trauma

FOR ARISTOTLE, tragedy flowed from the fatal flaw that marked the tragic hero. The flaw was pride — the pride of those who tried to overreach their human limitations to become like gods. Inexorably, the hero's tragic pride led to his downfall. In the twentieth century, the philospher Alfred North Whitehead defined tragedy in other terms — in the unfolding of nature. He wrote that tragedy "resides in the solemnity of the remorseless workings of things."[1] In this meaning, tragedy flows not from human agency but from the inevitability of the laws of nature, as in the eruption of a volcano or in an earthquake. Only incidentally do these events cause human misery and death.

The nuclear arms race evokes both meanings — the threat of tragedy linked to the pride that accompanies greatness, and the threat of tragedy linked to the incidental effects of harnessing nature. For nearly half a century the United States and the Soviet Union, divided by mistrust and conflicting ideologies, have confronted each other from behind a formidable arsenal of nuclear armaments. Each is determined to best the other, regardless of cost or sacrifice. Each country is sure that it is right and the other is wrong. Each devotes its greatest skills to exploiting science and technology in pursuit of victory. Although both countries say they are committed to stopping the nuclear arms race, arms control negotiations, even when successful, have done little more than tidy up the edges. Inexorably, the arms race moves forward.

After dropping its atomic weapons on Hiroshima and Nagasaki in 1945, the United States had no operational nuclear bombs and the Soviets had no bombs either. Forty-odd years later, the two superpowers between them have built an inventory of about fifty thousand nuclear warheads, some a thousand times more destructive than the Hiroshima bomb. Both sides deploy thousands of delivery vehicles carrying multiple nuclear warheads that can be launched from land-based sites, aircraft, or nuclear-powered submarines. As an ironic consequence of the effort to enhance national security, in three decades the United States went from absolute invulnerability to absolute vulnerability.

What would be the reaction of an expert in national security who, like Rip Van Winkle, awakened from a forty-year sleep in the late 1980s? What would he say about our national security now, as compared with the moment in 1945 when Harry Truman authorized the use of the nuclear bomb, ostensibly to end the war with Japan and save American lives?

The newly awakened Rip would surely be impressed with America's vitality so many years after the end of World War II. He would be stunned by the new technology — by the extent to which computers and electronic telecommunications have transformed our lives. He would be awed by the military applications of this technology, with its great leap forward in accuracy, sophistication, and destructive capability. He would be startled, perhaps alarmed, by the extent to which America's foreign policies have become linked to military force. Probably he would be impressed that the Soviet Union has survived Stalin's dictatorship, has consolidated a huge empire, and is managing to control it with a certain shaky stability. He would be amazed at Soviet military prowess, but depressed by the rigid authoritarianism of the system.

Above all, he would be dismayed by the erosion of U.S. national security, and utterly bewildered by the policy of spending billions of dollars annually on nuclear weapons, with the net effect of weakening our security further. Indeed, these policies would strike him as inexplicable and incredible. He would badger everyone who would listen with the same question: "How does our ability to wreak havoc on the Soviet Union add to our own security?" And, more shrilly, "What in the world is preventing the United States and the Soviet Union from putting an end to the insanity of a nuclear arms race? What has happened to the common sense of the American people? What has happened to the cunning and self-interest of the Soviet leaders? Has everyone gone berserk?"

The spectacle of our present national security policies would probably unhinge poor Rip. It does not have this effect on the rest of us only because Americans have found it so difficult to come to grips with the subject. An outmoded framework is deeply ingrained in the national thinking. Americans suspect that something is wrong with the choices they have been given, but they are unable to pin down the source of their uneasiness.

The principal flaw in the framework is that it harbors an obsolete idea, that of "nuclearized containment." This idea grew out of the merger of the two leading concepts of postwar American diplomacy, containment and deterrence.

Based on the European concept of a balance of power, the central idea of containment is that the Soviet Union has a "sphere of influence" and that the aim of U.S. policy is to draw a line around it and prevent the Soviets from expanding beyond it. In the late 1940s and early 1950s, when the United States enjoyed a virtual nuclear monopoly we began to use our nuclear arsenal to counterbalance Soviet superiority in numbers of troops available for combat. Gradually containment became "nuclearized"; that is, the United States came to depend on the threat of nuclear weapons to deter Soviet expansion. The use of the nuclear threat to achieve the political goal of containment is what former President Nixon calls "nuclear diplomacy."

These two concepts continue to form the core of U.S. policies of national security. In the chapters that follow, we discuss the origins of the policy of "nuclearized containment," we demonstrate why it is neither workable nor politically acceptable, and we sketch a new approach to national security drawn from our strategy of starting with the people.

2

Four Fateful Decisions

WHENEVER A SITUATION is inexplicable, it is useful to look back and ask, "How did it happen? How did we get here?" In retrospect, certain decisions prove to have been momentous. Let us begin by discussing four turning points that, in combination, have reinforced our national dependency on nuclear weapons.

Linking Containment with American Nuclear Weapons (1949–1954)

The policy of containment first took shape under Presidents Truman and Eisenhower. Enunciated in 1947 by George Kennan in a famous article in *Foreign Affairs,* the policy was modified by Dean Acheson and formalized by Paul Nitze in an important policy statement in 1950 (NSC-68).[1] These modifications brought to light a practical difficulty. Containment sought to confine the Soviet Union to the sphere of influence it had won through military occupation in the final days of World War II. Unfortunately, this goal demanded immense resources to prevent both Soviet military expansion and Soviet political subversion.

The postwar history of the containment policy, as historian John Gaddis points out, has oscillated between cutting back its scope when our resources have been limited and broadening it when the United States has felt particularly threatened by Soviet expansionism.[2] Kennan's original conception had limited objectives. Kennan de-emphasized the military side of containment and stressed instead the need to strengthen the economic and political structure of the nations around the periphery of the Soviet empire. (Our policy in Japan is a successful example of Kennan's idea.) The later versions of containment were more militarized. They expanded U.S. objectives and gave greater priority to confronting the Soviets with military force.

After the Korean War, an acute dilemma faced the United States. As usual after a military engagement, the country was eager to cut its military budget. President Eisenhower was concerned with costs, and his secretary of state, John Foster Dulles, was worried that containment left too much initiative to the adversary: the Soviet Union was free to choose its own timetable, arenas of confrontation, and preferred means for bringing the pot to a boil.

Nuclear weapons seemed the perfect solution. They were cheaper than conventional forces ("more bang for the buck"). Furthermore, greater strategic reliance on nuclear weapons would permit the United States to regain the initiative. We would be free to threaten to use nuclear weapons in response to Soviet aggression, leaving that nation to stew in uncertainty. Thus was born the policy of "massive retaliation" — the threat of escalation to nuclear war in response to Soviet use of conventional force. Dulles held that the United

States reserved the right to rely on nuclear retaliation, not only to counter a Soviet attack in Europe but also as a possible response to attacks elsewhere. In this formula, the threat of nuclear retaliation became the heart of containment.

In the 1950s most Americans supported this policy. A large majority (78 percent) knew that the United States enjoyed unchallengeable nuclear superiority (see Chart 1). This advantage filled Americans with serene security. We had total confidence in the sanity and peaceful intentions of our leaders. We believed the United States would never use nuclear weapons irresponsibly — that is, for any purpose other than as a last resort for survival. And we were confident that our superiority in nuclear weapons would deter the Soviets, or defeat them if they were insane enough to attack us or our allies. In that period fewer than two out of five Americans (38 percent) opposed using nuclear weapons to deter the Soviets (see Chart 2).

Nor in those years did Americans greatly fear the consequences of a nuclear war. In 1955 a Gallup poll found that only one out of four people (27 percent) believed that "all of mankind would be destroyed" by a nuclear war (see Chart 3). Opinion surveys showed that most Americans believed that

1 Postwar Awareness of a Nuclear Edge

Q. Do you think Russia has an edge on the U.S. in atom bombs and hydrogen bombs?

78%
The U.S. is superior

9%
Russia is superior

13%
Not sure

Source: Gallup, 1955.

2 Postwar Support for Nuclear Retaliation

Q. If one of our allies in Western Europe were attacked by the Russian army, do you think the U.S. would be justified in using atomic bombs against Russia?

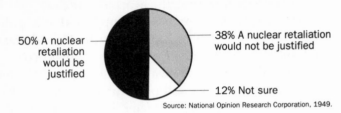

50% A nuclear retaliation would be justified

38% A nuclear retaliation would not be justified

12% Not sure

Source: National Opinion Research Corporation, 1949.

3 Postwar Doubt of Nuclear Destruction

Q. If an all-out atom and hydrogen bomb war should occur between Russia and the U.S., do you think all mankind would be destroyed or not?

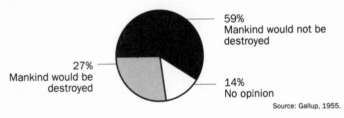

59% Mankind would not be destroyed

27% Mankind would be destroyed

14% No opinion

Source: Gallup, 1955.

nuclear weapons enhanced our national security. By a margin of two to one (59 percent to 29 percent), Americans saw nuclear weapons as a "good thing."[3]

In his 1946 "iron curtain" speech in Fulton, Missouri, Winston Churchill warned that the Soviets were determined to bring about "the indefinite expansion of their power and doctrines" in Eastern Europe unless the United States and its allies stopped them.[4] Believing the Soviet Union to be the principal threat to world peace, Americans saw their country as the world's policeman, with a nuclear billy club at the ready.

Reliance on nuclear weapons for containment was given a further boost by events in Europe. The North Atlantic Treaty Organization (NATO) was formed in 1949 to create a conventional armed force in Europe capable of defeating a Soviet attack. In Lisbon in 1952, NATO members affirmed that Western Europe would attend to its own defense and that Europeans themselves would accept responsibility for the security of Europe. The massive retaliation policy, announced in January 1954, changed all that. From that time, the response to Soviet aggression in Europe would be the prime responsibility no longer of Europeans but of those who had the nuclear weapons — Americans.

Policy analyst John van Oudenaren points out perceptively that this simultaneous "nuclearization" and "Americanization" of European security arrangements was one of the most fateful developments of the postwar period. Eventually it led the Western European countries around the periphery of the Soviet bloc to "see themselves as having less stake than the United States in countering the Soviet threat."[5] It created the opposite effect to the one envisioned by George Kennan. Instead of strengthening the will of these nations to defend themselves, it led them to see themselves almost as bystanders in a contest between two giants.

In retrospect, nuclearizing the containment policy was a bad habit into which the Western alliance fell. Each time the European members of NATO failed to live up to their commitments to strengthen their conventional armed forces (partly because of political resistance), it was all too easy to fall back on the American nuclear arsenal and its massive superiority (see David Schwarz, *NATO's Nuclear Dilemmas*, Washington, D.C: Brookings Institution, 1982). Since the NATO countries believed they posed no threat to the Soviet

Union, they felt no moral qualms about threatening nuclear retaliation. Out of hand they rejected the Soviet protest that the West was practicing nuclear blackmail.

The Soviets in turn quickly perceived that the link between containment and nuclear deterrence was the most vulnerable part of Western strategy. As the nuclear arsenals on both sides grew larger, the threat of retaliation came to lack credibility, because the retaliator would be committing suicide. Also, this policy frightened many Europeans, who worried that Western Europe, not the homelands of the two superpowers, might become the nuclear battleground. The Soviets set out to exploit this fear. They knew that for the Europeans, the blame for aggression counted less than the destructiveness of a nuclear war on their soil. The Europeans would end up just as dead whether the Soviets or the Americans were to blame.

Thus, in the early years of the postwar period a pattern was set that pointed U.S. policy directly toward its present impasse: institutionalizing the threat of nuclear retaliation and assuring mutual destruction if nuclear weapons were used. In the 1960s and 1970s the doctrine of mutual assured destruction (MAD) was elevated into an abstract scholastic theory endlessly elaborated by experts as if it were a splendid solution to the nuclear arms race rather than a morbid symptom of the problem. In the experts' discussions of the fine points of nuclear deterrence, humankind's disastrous ability to cover its most primitive emotions with a patina of rationality had found its ultimate form of expression.

The Unintended Consequences
of the Cuban Missile Crisis (1962–1974)

The second turning point was the Cuban missile crisis, in 1962. History books record it as a moment of triumph for young President Kennedy. In a brutal confrontation with the Soviets — a test of political will — the United States stood firm, and as then Secretary of State Dean Rusk put it, "the other guy just blinked." Unfortunately, the blink was to have lasting consequences. After the crisis, Soviet foreign minister Andrei Gromyko's deputy, Vasily Kuznetsov, warned his U.S. diplomatic counterpart, John McCloy: "You will never be able to do this to us again."[6] The Soviet leadership grew determined to strengthen its hand in any future test of wills over military might. From that time on, the Soviets would make any sacrifice needed to achieve nuclear parity with the Americans.

Normally the Soviet leadership avoids taking unnecessary risk. Soviet premier Nikita Khrushchev's impetuous attempt to change the balance of power overnight by smuggling intermediate-range ballistic missiles into Cuba and presenting the United States with a *fait accompli* was uncharacteristically risky. Apparently this mistake, above all others, cost Khrushchev his job.

In the Cuban missile crisis, the overwhelming nuclear superiority of the United States left the Soviet Union little choice but to back down. It confirmed for the Soviets one more time that nuclear weapons were the real power base in geopolitical relations. As they had done so often before, the Soviets made a tactical retreat, only to prepare themselves for a more favorable resolution next time.

In 1962 U.S. superiority in strategic nuclear weapons was indeed overwhelming. Five years earlier the Soviets had flight-tested an intercontinental ballistic missile (ICBM) and had launched Sputnik. In the 1960 presidential campaign there was much talk of a "missile gap" in favor of the Soviets, but after the election President Kennedy discovered that such a gap did not exist; we were decisively ahead in all categories. In 1955 the United States had introduced the first intercontinental jet bomber, the B-52, and at that time we

had a virtual monopoly in delivery systems as well as in overall numbers of weapons. In 1962 we had 229 ICBMs, as
compared with only 44 for the Soviets; they had about 155
strategic bombers, against 1300 for the United States[7] (see
Chart 4).*

4 Nuclear Arms Crossover Point

Total Strategic Nuclear Delivery Vehicles, 1956–1982*

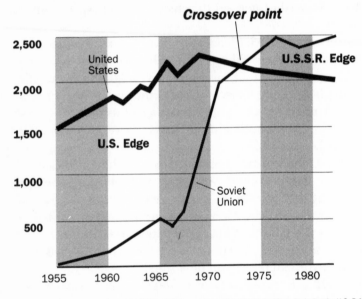

*Comprising ICBMs, SLBMs, and international range bombers (including the U.S. B-47).
U.S. bombers able to reach the Soviet Union only from foreign bases are excluded.
Source: Adapted from the Harvard Nuclear Study Group,
Living with Nuclear Weapons, 1983, by permission of Harvard University Press.

* These numbers are disputed by Randall Forsberg, founder of the nuclear
freeze movement. She states that in 1962, the Soviet Union had no fully operational ICBMs and that the United States had 2000, not 1300, strategic bombers
(600 B-52s and 1400 B-47s). Whichever set of numbers we rely on, the point
remains that in 1962, our military superiority was indeed overwhelming.

But after withdrawing their missiles from Cuba, the Soviets launched a huge military buildup. The Harvard Nuclear Study Group (six members of the Harvard faculty) concludes: "The kind of [nuclear] superiority that contributed to the outcome of the Cuban missile crisis disappeared forever as both sides pursued their nuclear buildup during the 1960s."[8] The nuclear arms race had begun in earnest.

For most of the 1960s the United States maintained its nuclear lead. But at the end of the decade, while America was preoccupied with the war in Vietnam, the Soviets began to reach parity in the most important dimension of nuclear capability: a second-strike, retaliatory force. By the early 1970s they had surpassed us in numbers of strategic nuclear delivery vehicles as well as in total megatonnage (although we maintained our lead in numbers of warheads). In 1974 they surpassed us in submarine-launched ballistic missiles and greatly strengthened their defensive capabilities against our intercontinental bombers. During this decade the United States began to "MIRV" its missiles, placing multiple warheads on each. This technological feat increased the number of strategic warheads in the U.S. arsenal, more than doubling them between 1970 and 1977. The Soviets responded in kind — and then some. By the end of the seventies, Soviet MIRVs had outpaced our own.[9] The public knew we had lost our edge (see Chart 5).

The "successful" resolution of the Cuban missile crisis thus accelerated the nuclear arms race. Perhaps the race would have accelerated anyway: the Soviets were determined to offset our decisive margin of superiority. But the consequences of the situation have surely made any future such crisis more dangerous. Tragically, after spending hundreds of billions of dollars on a military buildup, the American people were more exposed to danger than ever. With the new emphasis on intercontinental ballistic missiles, Americans became vulnerable to attack from abroad for the first time in history.

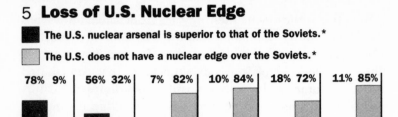

5 Loss of U.S. Nuclear Edge

■ The U.S. nuclear arsenal is superior to that of the Soviets.*

▢ The U.S. does not have a nuclear edge over the Soviets.*

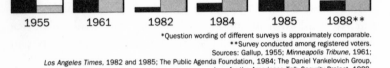

78% 9%	56% 32%	7% 82%	10% 84%	18% 72%	11% 85%
1955	1961	1982	1984	1985	1988**

*Question wording of different surveys is approximately comparable.
**Survey conducted among registered voters.
Sources: Gallup, 1955; *Minneapolis Tribune*, 1961;
Los Angeles Times, 1982 and 1985; The Public Agenda Foundation, 1984; The Daniel Yankelovich Group,
Inc., for the Americans Talk Security Project, 1988.

The Soviet "Rampage"
That Destroyed Détente (1975–1979)

We come now to what is perhaps the most unfortunate chapter in the chronicle of postwar relations between the United States and the USSR: the years when, in a series of miscalculations, détente was destroyed. For this setback many specialists believe the Soviets must accept major responsibility. From 1975 to 1979 the United States also made mistakes, but these appear minor compared to the shortsightedness of the Soviet leadership.

The policy of détente, as practiced first by the Nixon-Kissinger team, then by the Ford-Kissinger team, and then in a modified form by the Carter-Vance team, was a variant of the containment policy of maintaining the status quo against Soviet expansion. But it brought a different approach to containment. In the period before Nixon and Kissinger, military power (Korea, Vietnam) was stressed, as was economic aid to strengthen anticommunist governments. Now there was to be a greater emphasis on diplomacy and on peaceful "carrots" as well as "sticks" (for example, trade, the transfer of technology, and arms control agreements that would take pressure off the Soviet economy). Henry Kissinger has frequently stated that the détente policy was not a form of friendship but a strategy for relations among adversaries.

Détente was well received by the public. A Harris poll found widespread endorsement for the policy (defined as seeking out areas of agreement and cooperation with the Russians) (see Chart 6). But détente ran into difficulties almost from the start. Moves by Congress deprived the policy of its juiciest enticements, such as giving the Soviets most-favored-nation status in trade. The post-Vietnam decline in the defense budget and a diminishing public appetite for involvement in messy conflicts such as the one in Angola also weakened the threat aspect of détente. In the antimilitary mood of the United States between 1973 and the end of 1979, some of the modernization programs that the country was entitled to pursue under the SALT I agreement, such as the B-1 bomber and the MX missile, were stalled in favor of social priorities. The defense budget leveled off. Critics of

---

6 Public Views of Détente Before the Afghanistan Invasion

Q. Do you favor or oppose détente—that is, the U.S. and Russia seeking out areas of agreement and cooperation?

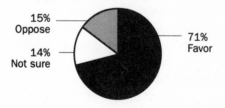

15% Oppose

14% Not sure

71% Favor

Source: Harris, 1978.

arms control and détente on the right of the political spectrum grew more active and vocal in their condemnation of the Soviet Union. In the aftermath of Watergate, Richard Nixon's prestige plummeted, and many aspects of détente were never implemented. Sovietologist Seweryn Bialer has observed that under détente the Soviets had neither anything to fear from U.S. displeasure nor anything to gain from U.S. approval.[10] In the end, the carrot-and-stick policy had few carrots or sticks.

It was in this context that the Soviets initiated a series of actions between 1975 and 1979 that Bialer characterizes as a "rampage." They supported their proxies, the Cubans, in Angola in 1975 and in Ethiopia in 1978. In December 1979 the Soviets invaded Afghanistan. This was the action that President Carter branded as "the worst threat to world peace since World War II." Bialer concludes that the Soviets interpreted détente as a license both for their own military buildup and for exploiting targets of opportunity in the Third World, and that in this pursuit of "peripheral gains" they sacrificed their central relation to the United States and humiliated America.[11]

In response to these actions and to mounting conservative criticism of the Soviets, American public attitudes toward détente soured. Majority support for the policy disappeared. The public came to believe that "during the 1970s, when we were trying to improve relations, the Soviet Union was secretly building its military strength" (see Chart 7). By 1980 the nation was divided on whether to support détente or return to a Cold War policy.

Why did the Soviets risk destroying détente, which it now insists is the only normal and correct policy between the two superpowers? Although there is no sure answer, there are several clues. Marshall Shulman, who was Secretary of State Cyrus Vance's chief adviser on Soviet affairs, recalls that dur-

7 The Public Sours on Détente

Q. Americans have different views about the Soviet Union and communism. [Do you agree or disagree with the view that] the Soviets used détente as an opportunity to build up their armed forces while lulling us into a false sense of security?

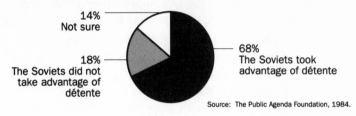

14%
Not sure

18%
The Soviets did not take advantage of détente

68%
The Soviets took advantage of détente

Source: The Public Agenda Foundation, 1984.

ing this period he encountered among Soviet officials an attitude of contempt for American policy makers. The Soviets interpreted our efforts to relax tensions in post-Watergate, post-Vietnam America as signs of weakness, and they saw the Carter Administration as both unreliable and weak.[12]

The Soviets had just completed the most formidable military buildup in their history. In their view, military parity entitled them to political prerogatives. As Nikita Khrushchev expressed it, "With equal forces, there must be equal rights and opportunities." They believed the international "correlation of forces" had shifted decisively in their favor. Détente, as they saw it, was based on U.S. acceptance of their more powerful status, on the relative decline of U.S. power, and consequently on a new balance of power in the world.

The Soviets made no attempt to disguise their intentions. Most experts agree with Paul Seabury, a scholar who is otherwise harsh in his judgment of the Soviets: "The Soviets, at least, cannot be blamed for deception regarding their aims and strategies. In their theoretical literature, little of which penetrated the American media, as well as in *Pravda*, in speeches, and in announcements and analyses, the Soviet leaders never, even at the height of détente, attempted such deception."[13] It is true, however, that our own political leaders oversold the American public on what could be expected of détente, which led to disillusionment and backlash.

Perhaps no episode in the troubled history of Soviet-American relations is as instructive. The Soviets mistook a momentary weakness in the American position for a permanent shift in the world balance of power in their favor, and exploited it with little regard for long-term consequences. They rejected the far-reaching proposals for arms reductions that Cyrus Vance brought to Moscow in 1977, on the premise that they were mere propaganda. They claimed to support détente, but what they meant by détente and what the Americans meant could hardly have been more disparate. By being utterly out of phase with each other, the two countries lost an opportunity to build a more constructive relationship.

Soviet action reveals the Soviet leaders of that period as surprisingly shortsighted and as subject to groupthink as any other bureaucrats. It demonstrates that the Soviets do not merely react to U.S. initiatives: they launch initiatives of their own, developed within their own framework of assumptions. One favorite assumption has been that strength flows only from military power. Their actions reinforced the conviction of average Americans that "the only thing the Soviets respect is force" and that the Soviets interpret conciliation as weakness.

Containment as a Crusade (1980–1983)

The fourth turning point was the U.S. reaction in the early 1980s to the Soviet military buildup of the 1960s and 1970s. This began in the last year of the Carter Administration. Mr. Carter's shock and disillusionment over the Soviet invasion

of Afghanistan had a profound effect on the public. His reaction fueled the feeling of impotence Americans were ex-
periencing from the futile effort to free our hostages in Iran
from Ayatollah Khomeini's grasp. Eventually our national
frustration gave rise to a new wave of American assertiveness,
a sharp increase in the defense budget, and the defeat of
Jimmy Carter at the polls in favor of a man who did not need
lessons in mistrusting the Russians. (As reasons for voting
against Jimmy Carter in 1980, voters cited "weakness in dealing with the Soviets" as second only to "poor performance in
managing the economy." [14]

Enter Ronald Reagan. In the years just before 1980, public
support for increased military spending had been gradually
growing. After the invasion of Afghanistan, it more than
doubled (see Chart 8). Reflecting the public mood, the Reagan Administration was determined to improve our strategic
position. It did so in several ways. First and foremost, it set
out to eliminate the military edge the Soviets had achieved
and to restore some form of American superiority (in Mr.
Reagan's words, "a margin of safety"). It rejected the Soviet

8 Support for Defense Spending, 1975–1980

Q. Are we spending . . . too little on the military, armaments, and
defense?

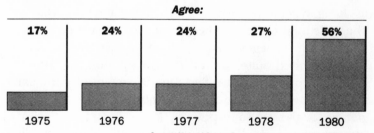

Agree:

17%	24%	24%	27%	56%
1975	1976	1977	1978	1980

Source: National Opinion Research Corporation (NORC), 1975–1980.

premise that military parity for the superpowers automatically translated into political equality.

After 1983 the centerpiece of U.S. policy became the Strategic Defense Initiative (SDI). An administration convinced that the Soviet "rampage" had to be not only halted but as far as possible reversed found in SDI a way to play from America's trump suit — high technology. SDI would springboard the United States into a whole new generation of military technology and thus push the global balance of forces, which had slipped so disastrously in the 1970s, back into America's favor.

In seeking to regain military superiority through SDI, the Reagan Administration found it necessary to discredit earlier arms control agreements with the Soviets that had been based on the principle of parity. The United States had negotiated no fewer than seventeen such agreements with the Soviets. The process had had its ups and downs, but for more than a generation it had been the centerpiece of U.S.-Soviet relations, and it was often the only cooperative element in an otherwise hostile relationship.

In its criticism of arms control agreements, the Reagan Administration was grandly nonpartisan: it blasted both political parties with equal fervor. In Mr. Reagan's first term, distaste for negotiating with the Russians became elevated to a principle called "non-negotiability." In his book *Deadly Gambits*, journalist Strobe Talbott describes the willingness of the Reagan team to dispense with negotiability — what the other side might accept — because it might constrain our side too much. Non-negotiability, Talbott says, reflects the belief that the United States should not do any business with the Soviets. In particular, it reflects the viewpoint of anti-Soviet hard-liners who believe that "the planet might not be big enough for the two superpowers." [15]

Simply stated, the Reagan Administration blamed the loss

of U.S. military superiority on arms control agreements with the Soviets. In 1982 Mr. Reagan stated that on balance, the "Soviet Union had won a definite margin of superiority in all important categories of weaponry." He explicitly faulted our arms control negotiations, especially the SALT agreements. Arms control agreements had lulled Americans into a sense of false security. In the words of the assistant secretary of defense, Richard Perle, such agreements are a "soporific . . . that puts our society to sleep."[16]

Mr. Reagan questioned the premise underlying all past arms control agreements. These agreements, he pointed out, aim not at reducing nuclear arms but at maintaining a stable balance of forces to strengthen deterrence. But nuclear deterrence doctrine, especially the doctrine of mutual assured destruction, is in Mr. Reagan's view barbaric, vengeful, and dangerous.

In his first term, Mr. Reagan also initiated a moral crusade against the Soviets. In contrast to the pragmatic approach taken by Ford and Kissinger, Mr. Reagan's policy was to present the struggle against Soviet communism to the public as a battle of good versus evil: the dominant image was that of an "evil empire" led by "Kremlin gangsters" intent on carrying out a plan for world domination, with only the United States standing in the way of Soviet success. Soviet communism was the moral equivalent of Nazism. The indictment was absolute.

In Soviet eyes, Mr. Reagan's policies were a clear effort to deny them the recognition that previous administrations (Republican and Democratic) had granted them as a legitimate global power. Relations between the two nations grew tense and hostile.

In his second term Mr. Reagan shifted his emphasis. He became less confrontational. He dropped the principle of non-negotiability. He moderated his rhetoric. He began to search for agreements that would reduce nuclear arms. But the effects of the first term were not easy to erase. The Cold War spirit had been rekindled, especially among conservatives. The United States had rearmed ideologically as well as militarily. In this context, SDI threatened to translate the ideological competition between the two systems — American capitalism and Soviet communism — into a nuclear arms race in space.

There is an important lesson to be drawn from these four episodes. It is that the competition between the United States and the Soviet Union should not be conceived of as a zero-sum game, where we win only if they lose and vice versa. In each case an apparent victory for one side was quickly transformed into diminished security for both. NATO's early shift to reliance on U.S. nuclear weapons handed the Soviets endless opportunities for stimulating nuclear war jitters in Europe, thus diminishing the West's real security. In resolving the Cuban missile crisis, the United States gained a short-term victory but fueled an arms race that escalated the dangers to both sides. In détente, the Soviets exploited what they perceived as an American political weakness for the sake of short-term advantages in Angola, Ethiopia, Afghanistan, and elsewhere. The result was an intense wave of anti-Soviet public sentiment in this country, which created the political conditions for continuing the arms race.

The Gap Between the Experts and the Public

ONE UNINTENDED EFFECT of these four decisions was to create a serious gap between the people, who are apprehensive about a nuclear arms race, and policy makers, who depend on our nuclear arsenal to protect America's strategic interests. In this chapter and the next, we explore the nature of the gap and what needs to be done to bridge it.

From the late 1940s to the late 1960s, the electorate and the experts enjoyed a shared outlook. Whatever the difficulties of the containment policy, lack of public support was not one of them. For two decades after World War II, a national consensus served both Democratic and Republican administrations faithfully and well. In one test after another — the Berlin airlift, the war in Korea, the Cuban missile crisis, the early years of the war in Vietnam — public support proved unswerving. But that consensus has long since evaporated. The public and the experts have parted company, and American policy has suffered accordingly.

The Expert Perspective

It is difficult for the public to receive guidance from the experts if the experts are divided and beset by contradictions. Unfortunately, U.S.-Soviet relations in the nuclear age are rife with this kind of trouble.

There has been a growing tendency in Washington to define the nuclear issue in ideological terms, which splits the experts into warring schools of thought. William Schneider of the American Enterprise Institute has described how ideology has polarized foreign policy elites.[1] At one end of the spectrum is the New Right, which has adopted a clear and pungent ideological stand. Its conservative world view is preoccupied with the conflict between the free West and the totalitarian East. It sees the United States as the leader of an anticommunist world alliance. It gives priority to military strength and is determined that the United States should regain the military superiority it once had. It looks back on détente with the Soviet Union in the 1970s as a period of weakness and immorality. In the pursuit of American global interests, it stresses the importance of U.S. initiatives, even hegemony; it does not shrink from military intervention in Third World conflicts to insure American victory and Soviet defeat.

At the other pole Schneider finds the "liberal internationalists." Their world view is dominated by North–South rather than East–West relations. They are deeply concerned with the economic plight of Third World nations and the growing disparity between haves and have-nots. They focus less on military power and more on economic and social relations and the need for mutual cooperation in an interdependent world. They fear the dangers of nuclear war far more than Soviet expansionism. For them, the immorality in American foreign policy was not détente with the Soviets but the Vietnam War. They too see the need for vigorous U.S. leadership, but in pursuit of very different goals and purposes.

Ironically, both groups fault the so-called eastern Establishment that dominated foreign policy in the postwar era until the 1970s. Both generate an antiestablishment populism that Schneider believes has been "the most important force in U.S. politics for the past twenty years."[2] As we shall see later, this same strain of populism also influences the public, but with different effects.

More important perhaps than the ideological split is a contradiction that lies at the very heart of U.S. policy, a contradiction bred by the marriage of containment and deterrence. In the early postwar years it was hidden from view because of America's nuclear superiority. But as our nuclear dominance has vanished, it has come to the fore. Our policy makers present containment and deterrence as different facets of the same policy, whereas they are actually in deep conflict with each other. The central purpose of deterrence is to prevent war. That is its only goal. The central purpose of containment, however, is to preserve a balance of power between the United States and the Soviet Union. If the Soviet Union crosses the lines we have drawn in the Western Hemisphere, in Europe, in the Middle East, and in Asia, the credibility of the policy requires us to respond forcefully, reserving to ourselves the right to escalate to nuclear war.

Drawing lines in the sand inevitably commits the United States to take strong action. The country went to war when North Korea crossed the line. It went to war to prevent a communist takeover in South Vietnam. It supported military action against Castro's Cuba (the Bay of Pigs), and threatened war with the Soviet Union in the Cuban missile crisis. It took military action in the Dominican Republic and in Grenada, and covert action to topple the left-leaning government of Premier Mossadegh in Iran (returning the shah to power) and the left-leaning government of President Allende in Chile. It is threatening the Sandinista government of Nicaragua with military action. The purpose of containment is not to avoid war; in fact, containment counts on the threat of war to achieve its objective.

From the standpoint of European history, there is nothing unusual about this policy—or about Soviet policies. They are traditional balance-of-power policies that Europeans have pursued for centuries. But in the nuclear age, that is precisely what is wrong with them. They lead, eventually, to war. Many arguments can be adduced in favor of balance-of-power diplomacy, but the low risk of war is not one of them. For centuries such policies have led Europe into war after war, and finally ruined Europe as the major seat of world power.

There is no way in which the United States can safely persist over the long haul in a policy that combines nuclear deterrence and containment. Either deterrence is undercut because of the built-in bias of the containment policy toward war, or containment is undercut because the threat of using nuclear weapons to achieve limited political goals is for all practical purposes an empty one. The worst of all policies is containment that does not contain and a threat of nuclear escalation that fuels the arms race and undermines deterrence. Hard-liner Aaron Wildavsky sums it up pithily: "Containment, pure and simple, is a losing game."[3]

It is important to understand that for many experts the present policy is more than a coldly calculated strategy for enhancing America's national security; it is a deeply felt emotional conviction, an implacable determination to restrain Soviet power. It is a question of ultimate values. Perhaps because our experts' desire to restrain the Soviets is so intense, they are blind to the way in which that desire pushes the

United States into military actions full of risks and distractions from our national goals.

Former President Nixon has described eight occasions when the United States has practiced nuclear diplomacy—that is, seriously considered using nuclear weapons to achieve a limited policy objective.[4] Prior to his presidency, he states, the United States deliberately used the bomb as a diplomatic stick to threaten our opponents in Korea (1952), Suez (1956), Berlin (1959), and Cuba (1962). As president, he personally considered using "the nuclear option" to end the war in Vietnam (1969). (Ultimately, he rejected this option as inefficient and as ruinous to his chances for improving relations with the Chinese and the Soviets.) He then considered using nuclear weapons in the Indo-Pakistani war in 1971, to prevent Indira Gandhi from annexing West Pakistan; in the 1973 Yom Kippur war, to counter Soviet leader Leonid Brezhnev's threat to intervene in the Middle East; and later to warn the Soviets that the United States would not tolerate a threatened Soviet attack against China's nuclear capability.

Ever since the Soviets achieved nuclear parity with the United States, the tug-of-war between the doctrines of deterrence and containment has grown more untenable. Nuclear diplomacy, as even its supporters concur, works well only when the United States has a decisive edge in strategic nuclear weapons. Once we lost that edge in the 1970s, nuclear diplomacy became impractical, and in recent years the United States has quietly dropped the practice of rattling its nuclear sabers.

Despite the increased danger, many defense experts believe that the United States has become so dependent on nuclear weapons that we cannot live without them. One such expert is Edward Luttwak, a Pentagon consultant and the author of *The Pentagon and the Art of War*.[5] In his view, the United States has consciously taken on the role of the world's major power. But, says Luttwak, Americans have failed to grasp the implications of this awesome responsibility. In Luttwak's view, it is impossible to be a great power without a great army. A great army means more than high-tech weapons and a nuclear arsenal; it requires large numbers of crack divisions manned by troops who have received long and tough training. The Soviet Union, according to Luttwak, understands this principle. The Soviets have a large army that serves as a serious, proficient instrument of their national policy, whereas America has failed to develop a great army or even to understand that we cannot implement our policies without one.

America's nuclear arsenal has compensated for the size and strength of the Soviet army to such an extent that, according to Luttwak, if arms control negotiations did succeed in eliminating nuclear weapons, the United States would have a disaster on its hands. To eliminate nuclear arms while leaving conventional arms in place would only "make the world safe for the Soviet army."[6] (As one top-ranking military expert inelegantly observed, nuclear arms have "saved our ass" and prevented nuclear war.)

Meanwhile, to continue with containment in a situation of nuclear parity is possible only if the United States is prepared to "outrisk" the Soviets. If we can't outgun them with nuclear weapons or conventional forces, we can run greater risks than they do. Our current policy is based on leaving all of our options on escalation open. It is assumed that the Soviets will behave themselves because they can never be sure what we will do or to what extent we have achieved what the Pentagon calls escalation dominance—the ability to dominate the military initiative on every step of the escalation ladder. The readiness of U.S. policy makers to outrisk the Soviets rests on the almost unbelievable truth that many of our experts have great confidence in the Soviet leadership and are prepared to trust it with our lives: they trust the Soviets not to risk everything they have built for some small gain.

Herein lies the great irony of the present situation. The more conservative and anti-Soviet our policy makers become and the more they denounce the Soviets as liars and masters of deception, the more confidence they appear to place in the restraint of the Politburo. Our most conservative anti-communists depend utterly on Soviet caution, rationality, prudence. We have replaced superiority in strategic nuclear forces with confidence in our "knowledge" of the psychology of our opponent. The current version of containment is a policy of second-guessing our opponents' intentions, based on assumptions about their perceptions of our perceptions. We have reduced the historic rivalry between American democracy and Soviet authoritarianism to a guess-ridden poker game, with human survival as the stakes.

In historian Barbara Tuchman's terms, this is a policy of exceeding folly. It is credible only if you believe that the United States is prepared to be reckless in the extreme. There are many theorists of American power (including Richard Nixon) who believe that it is desirable to have the Soviets perceive us as capable of irrationality. Such a belief, it is argued, keeps them off-balance. In the long run, however, this may be a very bad idea, because there is no practical way to confine the audience for irrationality to a few top Soviet leaders. Our allies and our own electorate are also audiences, and the effects on them are wholly negative. Our allies grow apprehensive about how responsible the United States is as a leader to whom they have entrusted their very survival. The American electorate receives exactly the wrong message— that playing nuclear chicken is acceptable. One part of the public is horrified, and comes to distrust the judgment of its government. The other part is reinforced in its macho response to international crises. In a contest between a skilled poker player, who is prepared to bluff and to risk everything on a single hand, and a skilled chess player, whose eye is on the outcome of the whole game, the chess player probably has the advantage.

The People's Viewpoint

Research conducted by the Public Agenda Foundation and the Center for Foreign Policy Development at Brown University contrasts the views of experts and the public. Neither group is homogeneous. Experts disagree among themselves about the strength of the Soviet Union, the intentions of its leaders, and the pros and cons of various weapons systems. The general public disagrees about the dangers of communist ideology and how much risk the United States should take to promote peace.[7]

Underlying these disagreements, however, is a core of agreement within each group, so that it is possible to speak of a public position and an expert position. The researchers found evidence of a serious and widening gap between the two, although there are some areas of agreement. For example, experts and the public agree about the devastating effects of nuclear war. The experts share the public's view that all-out nuclear war would be an unprecedented human catastrophe, with deaths in the hundreds of millions, and would threaten human survival. And both experts and the public perceive the Soviet Union as hostile to the interests of the United States. Most experts see the Soviet Union as an expansionist power determined to spread its influence in the world and extend its sphere of control. They regard the Soviets as repressive, obsessed with their internal security, and pursuing that security in ways that make other nations insecure. They believe the Soviet Union to be excessively dependent on military power to achieve its political objectives. This picture of the Soviets is shared by the public.

It is in calculating the risks of nuclear war that the public and the experts part company. In the past ten to fifteen years, the public has changed its mind about the danger of nuclear war and the degree to which our nuclear arsenal provides us with security. The American people no longer equate U.S. reliance on nuclear weapons with security, but equate it with *insecurity*. For the general public, the possibilities of a nuclear war are real, not abstract and remote. Young Americans in particular fear that such a war may break out in their lifetime.

With some exceptions, the experts reject the public's fears of nuclear war as unrealistic and even bordering on hysteria. They tend to minimize the risk of nuclear war as remote, improbable, and unrealistic. Their view is that deterrence works: it has worked for more than four decades, and it will go on working in the future, provided that we keep the balance of forces between ourselves and the Soviets reasonably stable.

This gap between expert and public opinion is one of the central political facts of our time. What has happened is that the public has changed its mind about nuclear weapons, whereas the defense experts have not. Let us track the change in the public's convictions and the reasons for it.

A Momentous Shift in Outlook

In the 1950s most Americans perceived nuclear weapons as furthering world peace. They feared the spread of communism more than they feared the dangers of nuclear war. Today most Americans continue to believe that Soviet communism poses a threat to values we cherish. But the majority have dramatically reversed themselves on the utility of nuclear weapons to counter that threat. Opposition to meeting a conventional Soviet attack with nuclear weapons has grown steadily over the years, from a 38 percent minority in 1949 to a whopping three out of four (74 percent) majority in 1984 (see Chart 9).

During the past few decades, three sets of public attitudes have shifted simultaneously.

1. *Loss of superiority.* In the 1950s most Americans believed the United States had nuclear superiority to the Soviets. In the 1980s the vast majority of Americans believe the United States has lost its margin of superiority. Fewer than one out of five Americans still believes that the United States has a nuclear edge over the Soviets (see Chart 5, p. 30). Moreover, Americans are overwhelmingly convinced (92 percent) that there is no way our country can regain its edge, since the Soviet Union "would simply keep building until they caught up."[8]

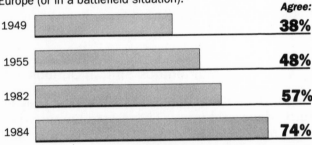

9 Resistance to U.S. Use of Nuclear Weapons

Q. The U.S. should not use nuclear weapons if the Russians invade Western Europe (or in a battlefield situation).*

Agree:

1949	**38%**
1955	**48%**
1982	**57%**
1984	**74%**

*Question wording of different surveys is comparable.
Sources: National Opinion Research Corporation, 1949 and 1955;
CBS News/*New York Times*, 1982; The Public Agenda Corporation, 1984.

2. *Consequences of nuclear war.* At the same time, as we have noted, Americans have grown convinced that a nuclear war would be so devastating that "all humankind would be destroyed." Only one out of four held this view in the mid-fifties: by the mid-eighties, the number had swollen to nine out of ten (see Chart 10).

There is no *logical* connection between these two views. Whether the United States has nuclear superiority to the Soviets has little bearing on the devastation of a nuclear holocaust. But interviews show a *psychological* link. For most Americans, U.S. nuclear superiority was a source of safety and comfort. The public treasures the conviction that our country is prudent in its use of power: as long as America had the upper hand, the damage could be contained. But once America lost its edge — and therefore lost control over the arms race — it also lost the ability to limit destruction.

3. *A change of heart about nuclear weapons.* As a consequence of the loss of invulnerability, Americans no longer see nuclear weapons as contributing to our national security. In-

---

10 The Public Changes Its Mind About Nuclear War

Q. If an all-out atomic and hydrogen bomb war should occur between Russia and the U.S., do you think all mankind would be destroyed?

Yes, complete destruction would occur:

1955   **27%**

Q. Do you agree or disagree with the following statement? "There can be no winner in an all-out nuclear war; both the U.S. and the Soviet Union would be completely destroyed."

Agree:

1987   **83%**

Source: Gallup.

stead, they now see nuclear weapons as a "bad thing" undermining the national security. The research findings are un-
ambiguous: instead of the two-to-one margin in favor of
nuclear weapons that prevailed in the 1950s, only one out of
four voters now sees nuclear weapons as a "good thing" for
our national security, as compared to the two-thirds majority
(65 percent) who now disapprove of them (see Chart 11).

Why have Americans changed their views so sweepingly?
Many factors have contributed. The Physicians for Social Responsibility, the Union of Concerned Scientists, the nuclear
freeze movement, and other groups have mounted public
information campaigns dramatizing the destructiveness of
nuclear war. Scientists who study the havoc that nuclear ex-
plosions would wreak on the world's atmosphere and food
supplies have persuaded the Pentagon as well as the public
that the danger is serious. Respected senior statesmen, including George Kennan, Robert McNamara, Jerome Weisner, Thomas J. Watson, and others, have preached the
dangers of our nuclear policies to all who will listen.

But the clearest message has come from the dawning public realization of a new reality. In the 1950s, when public
views about nuclear weapons were positive, the United States

---

11 Public Views About Nuclear Weapons, 1949 and 1982

Q. Do you think it was a good or bad thing that the atomic bomb
was developed?

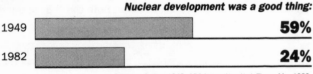

Nuclear development was a good thing:

1949 — **59%**

1982 — **24%**

Sources: Gallup, 1949; CBS News/*New York Times*, May 1982.

was virtually invulnerable to destruction. (The Soviets had nuclear bombs but did not have delivery systems.) What has rendered us vulnerable is the Soviet buildup of large numbers of intercontinental ballistic missiles in the 1960s and 1970s, and the lack of a viable defense against them.

The explanation for the public's change in outlook is at bottom simple. Our attitudes have changed because the reality has changed. We didn't fear nuclear weapons when they could not hurt us. Now that we are vulnerable to instant destruction, we do fear them. The great psychological appeal of SDI is that it addresses this vulnerability: it holds out the promise of restoring our former security.

A Latent Dissatisfaction

As a result of the public's change of mind about nuclear weapons, the political context for U.S.-Soviet relationships has also changed. Instead of a strong public mandate for our policies, there is a widespread, latent dissatisfaction. The public's growing awareness of U.S. vulnerability has created a vague but mounting uneasiness that something is amiss in our national security policies. And the public suspects that no one knows what to do about it.

Latent dissatisfaction does *not* mean that the public is opposed to all aspects of U.S. nuclear policy — as it was opposed, for example, to U.S. policy in the later stages of the Vietnam War. The present mood is more fluid and diffuse; the dissatisfaction has not yet focused itself.

Public uneasiness is also caused by the inconsistencies in our current policy. On the one hand, our leaders state that a nuclear war cannot be won and must never be fought. Soviet leaders make similar statements. But whatever they claim to the contrary, both nations proceed daily as if they could always fall back on nuclear war as an option — a destructive one, but a practical option nonetheless. Despite the rhetoric, both maneuver ceaselessly for tiny strategic advantages. The public does not know the details, but fears what is being done behind the scenes; these actions fill people with dread.

Public apprehension is expressed in various ways. In interviews average Americans say things like "if both sides keep making these weapons, sooner or later they are going to be used," and "Even if it's all the Russians' fault, if there's a nuclear war, we are going to be just as dead as they are."[9] Significantly, most Americans do *not* believe that responsibility should be laid exclusively at the Soviets' door. A majority agree that the United States is also at fault. In repeated surveys (the most recent in 1988), more than three out of four voters concur with statements such as "the United States has to accept some of the blame for the tension in U.S.-Soviet relations in recent years" (see Chart 12).

Latent dissatisfaction is also clearly reflected in the public's misunderstanding of present U.S. policies. Survey research shows that the American people are remarkably uninformed about what U.S. nuclear policy actually is, and it suggests that as they learn more about it, they will grow less supportive. Consider public attitudes toward first use of nuclear weap-

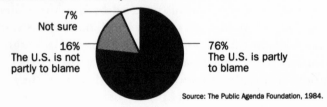

12 **Blame for U.S.-Soviet Tensions**

Q. Do you agree or disagree with the following statement? "The U.S. has to accept some of the blame for the tension that has plagued U.S.-Soviet relations in recent years."

7%
Not sure

16%
The U.S. is not
partly to blame

76%
The U.S. is partly
to blame

Source: The Public Agenda Foundation, 1984.

ons. The long-standing policy of the United States is to be prepared to use nuclear weapons before the Soviets do to deter any attack on our allies by conventional forces. The idea is to keep the Soviets fearful that if they encroach on Western Europe by conventional means — in West Berlin or West Germany, for example — they face the might of the U.S. nuclear arsenal. The rationale for the policy is that this threat is a powerful deterrent to such Soviet encroachment, and a much more economical one than an effort to match Soviet conventional forces on the European mainland with Western ones.

But by contrast, most Americans (69 percent) believe the United States is committed *not* to use nuclear weapons unless they are used against us first. The survey data further suggest that if the electorate did understand existing policy, they would be opposed to it. Fewer than one out of five Americans (18 percent) believes that our policy should be to retaliate with nuclear weapons against a non-nuclear attack on our allies. As is often the case on issues charged with anxiety, most Americans think our policy actually is what they would like it to be (see Charts 13 and 14).

The history of President Reagan's performance ratings in opinion polls gives another glimpse of latent dissatisfaction at work. In 1983 the economy began to recover from the severe recession of 1981–1982. As it did so, Mr. Reagan's "approval ratings" rose sharply. By late 1983 a majority of voters expressed confidence in Mr. Reagan in 22 out of 23 categories measured by *Time*.[10] The one aspect of the Reagan presidency that disturbed the majority was the fear that Mr. Reagan might lead us into war with the Soviet Union. Because of the nuclear threat, this concern deeply troubled the voters. Mr. Reagan's popularity regarding the economy had reached an unprecedented crest, yet his perceived cowboy attitudes toward nuclear weapons marred his record.

In early 1984, responding to the public's concerns, Mr.

13 Public Misperception of "First Use" Policy

Q. Do you agree or disagree with the following statement? "It is current U.S. policy to use nuclear weapons against the Soviets if they invade Europe or Japan with soldiers and tanks, even if they don't use nuclear weapons."

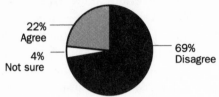

22% Agree

4% Not sure

69% Disagree

Source: The Public Agenda Foundation, 1984.

14 Opposition to "First Use"

Q. Do you agree or disagree with the following statement? "By the 1990s, it should be U.S. policy to use nuclear weapons against the Soviets if they invade Europe or Japan with soldiers or tanks, even if they don't use nuclear weapons first."

18% U.S. policy should be "first use"

5% Not sure

77% U.S. policy should not be "first use"

Source: The Public Agenda Foundation, 1984.

Reagan declared himself more receptive to negotiations with the Soviets. The public response was overwhelmingly positive.[11] By moving from confrontation to a more cooperative posture, Mr. Reagan corrected the single major deficiency in his standing, an action that prepared the ground for his decisive electoral victory later that year.

Perhaps the most revealing glimpse into public attitudes comes in connection with the people's response to the summit meeting between Mr. Reagan and Mr. Gorbachev in Iceland in October 1986. When the talks broke down, the administration's initial reaction was to treat the summit as a policy failure and to search for a public relations strategy that would make the failure look like a success. But soundings of public opinion afterward revealed a different response. The public interpreted the meeting not as a breakdown but as a breakthrough! Instead of being disheartened by the failure to reach agreement, the American people reacted strongly and favorably to the discussions between the two leaders. They liked the idea that their president was willing to break through the rigid limitations imposed by thirty years of expert negotiation on arms control.

The values of the American public gave warm support to the insight (almost an epiphany) that bold solutions to the arms race had almost been reached in that brief but fateful meeting. All at once, obstacles that specialists had for decades been treating as insurmountable were swept aside in favor of a vision of mutual security that the two leaders, both stubborn men wedded to the security of their respective nations, presented to each other. After the Iceland "defeat," Mr. Reagan received the highest approval rating in his presidency for "handling relations with the Soviet Union"! It was in effect his last hurrah before the Iran-contra fiasco.

What the public responded to in this case was a vision of genuine leadership: the president was seen as cutting through the mind-numbing technicalities of the nuclear arms race, removing the ideological blinders, and working at a fundamental level toward broad-ranging solutions. Shortly thereafter the Reykjavik summit receded into the background. But something had happened that changed irreversibly the conditions for coping with the nuclear issue. Once freed from its prison, the human imagination cannot be easily recaptured. Since the Iceland summit, all discussions of the arms race have had to consider bolder solutions than before.

We are not suggesting that the agreement discussed in Reykjavik was the correct solution; it had obvious drawbacks for the United States. But it underscored the point that the American public is prepared to embrace more far-reaching solutions to the nuclear threat than its leaders have been willing to address for the past forty years. Such signs indicate that people are unhappy with the current U.S. posture on nuclear weapons but have not yet decided on an alternative. As a result, public opinion remains at the level of mass opinion, volatile and ill-informed. The missing element—and it is a grievous policy failure — is alternatives to existing policies. Until such alternatives are offered, public support will continue to show signs of disarray and instability.

4

Public Values on Which Consensus Can Be Built

IF THE ELECTORATE has changed its mind about nuclear weapons, why have the country's policy makers, who know so much more about the subject, failed to change their minds? Do the experts know something the public does not know? Is the public exaggerating the destructiveness of nuclear war, having been brainwashed by scary films and TV shows and the peace movement? Is the security of the United States less vulnerable than the public fears? Do the experts have the situation in firmer control than appearances would suggest? What *does* account for the disparity?

As we suggested earlier, what divides the experts from the public is not information but a difference in values. The public brings one framework of values to the threat, the experts another.

The Experts' Framework

The experts' view is that although maintaining a balance of mutual terror may not be an appealing prospect, it is a practical solution to the problem of nuclear arms. Besides, in the experts' view, there are no alternatives. We cannot un-invent nuclear weapons; we cannot put the genie back in the bottle. Nor can we risk unilateral reductions in arms, because this would only induce the Soviets to fill the vacuum. The Soviet leaders are pragmatic, cautious, and rational: they are not going to risk everything on nuclear confrontation with the United States. The experts believe that if we maintain our strength and political will, we can contain and deter Soviet power.

Since the threat of nuclear war is remote, U.S. policy must not be paralyzed by timidity. If we demonstrate to the Soviets that we have the nuclear jitters and will never, under any circumstances (except nuclear attack by them), use our nuclear weapons, then our policies will lose their credibility. Besides, it is always best to keep the Soviets guessing. We must take advantage of the element of uncertainty in our calculations. This will help to keep the Soviets on the cautious side, since the consequences of a nuclear confrontation are so dire.

This is a plausible argument, and the American people have yet to hear a compelling alternative to it. Yet even without choice, they remain unconvinced.

Survey findings show that the public and the experts bring a different time frame to the issue. Among policy makers, there are only a few (such as elder statesman Paul Nitze) who take the long view. The day-to-day responsibilities of most policy makers incline them to a short-term viewpoint: their preoccupation is with next year's defense budget, next month's negotiations in Geneva, next week's congressional hearings, the next election. In seeking tactical advantages over the Soviets (or, for that matter, over the State Department or the House Armed Services Committee), they are tempted to think in terms of weeks and months rather than decades and generations.

The Public Framework

The general public is spared the day-to-day maneuvering. The American people bear no responsibility for policy decisions. They do not have to struggle for tactical advantage against clever and determined opponents. Ironically, on most issues (such as trade policy), their attention span is shorter than that of the experts. But on nuclear weapons, the public's perspective is remarkably long-term. Americans in their twenties think of their remaining lifespan — a half century or more — and wonder whether their lives will be cut short by nuclear catastrophe. Strikingly, 50 percent of Americans under thirty fear that nuclear war will come in their lifetime.[1] Older Americans think in terms of their children and grandchildren and pray that they will not know the terror of nuclear Armageddon. Two thirds of Americans of all ages (68 percent) hold the commonsense conviction that if both sides keep building newer and more powerful weapons, sooner or later they will be used (see Chart 15).

Nor does the public share the experts' surprising view of the Soviet leaders as rational. For the public, the Soviets are not cautious and reasonable, pressing forward only when the odds favor them, holding back when the risk is too great. The public assumption is that the Soviet leaders, being prey to human error and passion, might make some dreadful mis-

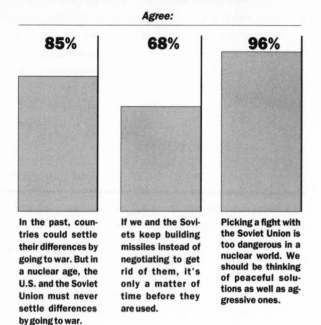

Agree:

85%	68%	96%
In the past, countries could settle their differences by going to war. But in a nuclear age, the U.S. and the Soviet Union must never settle differences by going to war.	If we and the Soviets keep building missiles instead of negotiating to get rid of them, it's only a matter of time before they are used.	Picking a fight with the Soviet Union is too dangerous in a nuclear world. We should be thinking of peaceful solutions as well as aggressive ones.

Source: The Public Agenda Foundation, 1984.

calculation or launch an adventure that no one could then control.

The experts and the public may each be correct from their own perspective. In the short term (for example, the next five years), the danger of nuclear war probably is slight, and the United States may gain some advantages by taking risks in the nuclear arms race. But the public is correct in its assumption that in the long run, a breakdown of nuclear-based deterrence is virtually inevitable. History demonstrates that it is irresponsible to risk everything on a policy that cannot tolerate a single breakdown, ever. Every lesson of history shows that fallible humans, armed with weapons of immense destructiveness, will not maintain a clear-headed vision of their own security, will not be able to resist provoking their enemies, will not show steadfast prudence, rationality, and restraint. To count on an unfailing reasonableness that will endure consistently for generations as the containment policy does, is to expect humans not to be human.

A policy that depends on nuclear diplomacy creates a crippling confusion of goals. Luttwak's assertion that eliminating nuclear weapons on both sides — a dream that inspires millions of people all over the world — would be a disaster for the United States because it would "make the world safe for the Soviet army" is a terrible indictment of present policy. What Luttwak is saying, in effect, is that the more we reduce our nuclear arms in concert with the Soviets (as in theory we are trying to do), the more we leave our containment policy toothless and ineffectual.

There is no way to paper over the gravity of the conflict between experts and public. Either the American people must learn, as in the past, to love the bomb, or the experts must abandon nuclearized containment.

It is worth emphasizing again that the gap between experts and public is not caused by expert knowledge and public ignorance. Information is not what separates the two. It is more fundamental, a question of role, perspective, and values. The role of defense experts is to get the most mileage from existing policy; it is their job to find tactical advantages for the United States in the existing situation. Paradoxically, the very destructiveness of nuclear weapons has given the experts an illusory sense of security. They assume that because nuclear weapons are suicidally destructive, no sane nation would think seriously of using them. These experts have a double vision of the Soviets. They see them both as an implacable enemy of the United States and as rational people who would not risk destruction for tactical gains. Consequently, it seems relatively safe to take chances.

From the public viewpoint, tactical advantages count for little when weighed against the long-term threat of human destruction through nuclear war. Also, though the people fear communism, they are less ideologically committed to a struggle-to-the-death with it than many ideologues among the experts and policy makers are.

This situation — the public leaning one way, official policy makers leaning another — is the worst possible basis for a national policy that is supposed to walk surefootedly between the twin threats of nuclear war and Soviet expansionism. To be successful, such a policy must have the full support of the public. The American people should know in general terms what the policy is, agree with its objectives, endorse its strategy, and give their trust and confidence to those leaders whom they charge with its execution. Otherwise the policy is built on sand.

The United States needs a stable policy on which our allies *and* our adversaries can depend. We need to reassure our allies that the commitments they undertake for the common defense at the behest of the United States will not be undermined by political change. And the Soviets need to be convinced that they cannot gain unilateral advantages simply by outwaiting a policy they do not like on the assumption that if they hang tough, the U.S. position will change.

Having a foreign policy supported by a strong public consensus is indispensable to the national security of the United States. How can such a national consensus be created? Is any policy capable of winning support from, say, two thirds or more of the electorate, excluding only those voters at the extremes of the political spectrum? What criteria would such a policy have to meet? The findings of research on public values suggest an answer to these important questions.

Coming to Judgment

We stated in the Introduction that on matters about which Americans hold firm convictions, their responses remain constant, even when questions in opinion polls vary in their wording. For example, a firm consensus exists on the dangers of nuclear war. No matter how the questions are worded, the answers come back unequivocally: nuclear war is unwinnable, unsurvivable.

On other matters, when Americans have not yet worked out how they feel, public attitudes are much more unstable. An example is public views on verification of arms control agreements. When asked what risks would be acceptable to them, a majority of Americans (56 percent) say that it would be an acceptable risk for the United States to "sign an arms control agreement with the Soviets even if foolproof verification can't be guaranteed."[2] But in response to a question worded in a slightly different fashion, the majority also endorse a contradictory response, that "unless the Soviets agree to on-site inspection, we should refuse to sign any arms control agreements with them."[3] The presence of such contradictions is a sure sign that the public has not yet come to a final judgment.

On attitudes toward nuclear arms and Soviet relations, the American people have formed a stable judgment on four key principles or values that do command a firm public consensus. To be politically acceptable to the electorate, U.S. foreign policy must adhere to them: they form the criteria for shaping a policy capable of winning long-term public support.

REDUCING VULNERABILITY TO NUCLEAR WAR

As we have seen, there exists a firm public consensus that a nuclear war would be suicidal and that the danger of such a war is real. More than three fourths of the public are persuaded that

- "there can be no winner in an all-out nuclear war; both the U.S. and the Soviet union would be completely destroyed" (83 percent).[4]
- "a limited nuclear war is nonsense; if either side were to use nuclear weapons, it would turn into all-out nuclear war" (83 percent).[5]
- we can "no longer be certain that life on earth would continue" after a nuclear war (83 percent).[6]
- there "is nothing on earth that could ever justify the all-out use of nuclear weapons" (79 percent).[7]

Any policy that increases the risk of nuclear war will be interpreted by the public as making the country more vulnerable and reducing its security. It is impossible to win stable, consensus-level support for a policy that does not address this fear.

NEGOTIATING WITH THE SOVIETS IN GOOD FAITH

Whatever their mistrust of Soviet leadership and their support for U.S. military power, Americans are convinced that the only way to resolve the arms race is through negotiation. The prospect of nuclear war is so threatening that people see no option other than negotiation:

- "Picking a fight with the Soviet Union is too dangerous in a nuclear world. We should be thinking of peaceful solutions as well as aggressive ones" (96 percent).

- "In the past, countries could settle their differences by going to war. But in a nuclear age, the U.S. and the Soviet Union must *never* settle their differences by going to war" (85 percent).
- "If we and the Soviets keep building missiles instead of negotiating to get rid of them, it's only a matter of time before they are used" (68 percent). (See Chart 15, p. 60.)

Americans' commitment to negotiation grows out of a pragmatic willingness to accept the Soviets as adversaries with whom it is possible to coexist. Although Americans don't like either communism or the Soviet leadership, they believe we can share the planet with the Soviets. About three fifths of the public (59 percent) endorse the view that "we should live and let live; let the communists have their system and we ours. There's room in the world for both" (see Chart 16).

NOT DEPENDING ON SOVIET GOOD WILL

Americans are deeply suspicious of policies that depend on trusting the Soviet leadership. They no longer feel threatened by communist ideology, as in the McCarthy era, in the

16 **Support for "Live and Let Live"**

Q. Do you agree or disagree with the following statement? "We should live and let live; let the communists have their system and we ours. There's room in the world for both." *

2%
Not sure

39%
No, there is not room in the world for both systems

59%
Yes, there is room in the world for both systems

*Survey conducted among registered voters.
Source: The Daniel Yankelovich Group, Inc., for the Americans Talk Security Project, 1988.

1950s; there is no widespread fear that communism will spread in the United States or even among our European allies. Also, most Americans have come to believe that the United States can exist on good terms with Marxist governments. More than seven out of ten voters (71 percent) concur that "we can get along with communist countries; we do it all the time." Here our experience with China, Yugoslavia, and Poland has been particularly influential. Americans now see that the communist world is not monolithic and that some communist countries do not constitute a threat. More than eight out of ten voters (83 percent), for example, endorse the view that "our experience with communist China proves that our mortal enemies can turn into countries we can get along with" (see Chart 17).

17 Support for Getting Along with Communist Countries

Q. We can get along with communist countries; we do it all the time.

4%
Not sure

17%
Disagree

71%
Agree

Q. Our experience with communist China proves that our mortal enemies can turn into countries we can get along with.

9%
Not sure

12%
Disagree

83%
Agree

Source: The Public Agenda Foundation, 1984.

Although Americans like and admire the Russian people, they are wary of the Soviet leaders and their goals. Nearly nine out of ten believe that the Russian people are not as hostile to the United States as their leaders are, and in fact that the Russians could be our friends if their leaders had a different attitude.[8] In the past few years, of course, initiatives led by Secretary-General Gorbachev have significantly moderated Americans' cold war attitudes. In 1988 the public held the view, by 51 percent to 38 percent, that the Soviet Union was more interested in "maintaining peaceful relations with the West" than in "achieving global domination" for communism. This is a big change from 1984, when a large majority of the American people (58 percent) believed that the primary foreign policy goal of the Soviet Union was global domination.[9]

Attitudes toward the Soviets fluctuate with events. But the key point is that mistrust of the Soviet Union is widespread and deeply rooted. It will not dissipate quickly. Americans suspect that in pursuit of its goals, the Soviet government has taken advantage of past friendly gestures, and that it will do so again in the future.

- Eighty-two percent believe the Soviets are constantly testing us, probing for weakness, and are quick to take advantage whenever they find any.
- Seventy-three percent believe that the "Soviets treat our friendly gestures as weakness."
- Sixty-six percent believe that "the Russians cannot be trusted to keep their word on agreements made in a summit meeting between Mr. Reagan and Mr. Gorbachev."
- Sixty-four percent believe the Soviets "lie, cheat, and steal—they'll do anything to further the cause of communism."

- Sixty-one percent believe that "the Soviets have cheated on just about every treaty and agreement they have ever signed" (see Chart 18).

MAINTAINING U.S. MILITARY STRENGTH

Americans are also convinced that the United States should operate from a position of military strength. Although Americans do not think it is possible to *win* the arms race, they do believe that it is possible to *lose* it if we allow the Soviets to gain an advantage. More than two thirds (71 percent) believe that "the U.S. should continue to develop new and better nuclear weapons because technological breakthroughs might make those we now have obsolete." By a clear majority (57 percent to 37 percent), Americans believe that "the U.S. must not lose the arms race. We must continue to develop new and better nuclear weapons." There is virtual unanimity that America's nuclear strength must be at least equal to that of the Soviet Union (see Chart 19).

This insistence on American military power grows directly out of people's mistrust of the Soviet leaders. There is a widespread feeling that American weakness might lead to Soviet expansion, because the Soviets would try to exploit that vulnerability. Large majorities believe that

- "if we are weak, the Soviet Union, at the right moment, will attack us or our allies in Europe or Japan" (64 percent).
- "the Soviets respond only to military strength" (55 percent in 1988, down from 67 percent four years earlier). (See Chart 19 on page 70.)

These four sets of values are difficult to encompass in a single, unified policy. But difficult or not, they constitute the

Agree:

82%

The Soviets are constantly testing us, probing for
weakness, and they're quick to take advantage
whenever they find any. (1984)

73%

The Soviets treat our friendly gestures as
weaknesses. (*Time*, 1983)

66%

The Russians cannot be trusted to keep their word on
agreements made in a summit meeting between Mr.
Reagan and Mr. Gorbachev. (1985)

64%

The Soviets lie, cheat and steal—they'll do
anything to further the cause of communism.
(Americans Talk Security Project, 1988)

61%

The Soviets have cheated on just about every
treaty and agreement they have ever signed.
(1984)

Sources: Yankelovich, Skelly and White, statements 2 and 3; The Daniel Yankelovich Group, Inc.,
statement 4; The Public Agenda Foundation, statements 1 and 5.

present boundaries of political acceptability. Any policy seen
as diminishing our security through heightening the risk
of nuclear war, or weakening our military strength, or being naive about the Soviet leadership, or failing to negotiate in good faith with our Soviet opponents to prevent blow-
ing each other up, would be rejected by the American electorate.

Public Support of U.S. Military Strength

Agree:

71%

The U.S should continue to develop new and better
nuclear weapons because technological breakthroughs might make those we have now obsolete.

64%

If we are weak, the Soviet Union, at the right
moment, will attack us or our allies in Europe and
Japan.

57%

The U.S. must not lose the arms race. We
must continue to develop new and better nuclear
weapons.

55%

The Soviets respond only to military strength.

Source: The Public Agenda Foundation, 1984, statements 1 and 3; Market Opinion
Research, for the Americans Talk Security Project, 1988, statement 2; The Daniel
Yankelovich Group, Inc., for the Americans Talk Security Project, 1988.

How firm are these convictions? All four can be modified
to some degree by events or by determined leadership. Some
conservatives, for example, believe that the country is being
brainwashed by the mass media and the peace movement
about the dangers of nuclear war. They want to see less attention given to these dangers, on the grounds that growing
public nervousness will undermine our current policies. At
the other end of the political spectrum, some liberals see a
contradiction between our present military policies and na-

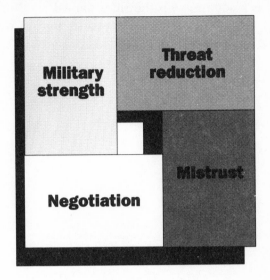

tional security. They believe that we would be much more secure with lower levels of military strength.

Whatever the merit of these arguments, it is unlikely that these four criteria will weaken in the immediate future. It is more realistic to regard them as a challenge from the public to its political leaders. "Devise for us," the American people are saying, "a policy in which a strong America, keeping faith with our deepest convictions, has the maturity to negotiate hardheaded mutual security arrangements with our opponents that will prevent our differences from escalating into nuclear war." This point of view is not irrational or even unreasonable.

Together these four criteria can be regarded as boundary lines of political acceptability. Schematically, they can be visualized as a square, with the sides named (1) threat reduction, (2) military strength, (3) mistrust, and (4) negotiation (see Chart 20 on previous page).

How the Public Judges Policies

THE FOUR VALUES that form the boundaries of political acceptability clearly demonstrate the terms and conditions for
a new national consensus. As we have shown, only a policy
that matches these four values can hope to win enduring
public support. As the data presented in this chapter show,
present policies and options fail the test. Those policies that
fail on all four values are utterly rejected by the public. The
policies that express some of the public's values but not others apparently enjoy public support, but the support is not
firm. As soon as someone proposes counterarguments that
call attention to the values that are scanted, the support
erodes.

In this chapter we test five policies against the public's values. One of them, unilateral disarmament, violates all the
values and has no political support. The others — traditional
arms control, détente, nuclear freeze, and SDI — meet some
values but not others. As a result they all have inconsistent
and fluctuating support. None has the potential to command

the long-term political support needed to reverse the nuclear arms race.

Unilateral Disarmament

The strongest possible aversion attaches to accusations that the United States is the culprit in the arms race, with the Soviets merely reacting to U.S. initiatives. Americans are wary of setting an example by reducing U.S. military strength, especially in nuclear arms, in the expectation that the Soviets will follow, and are suspicious of a preoccupation with the nuclear threat to the exclusion of any concern about the threat of Soviet expansion.

Unilateral approaches, more characteristic of the European peace movement than of American thinking, violate all four boundaries of political acceptability. Americans see unilateral disarmament as increasing the risk of nuclear war, because we would be weakening our deterrent while the Soviets maintained theirs, thereby tempting them to blackmail us or even to attack us because of our increased vulnerability. Americans regard this approach as diminishing our military strength, as being insufficiently wary of the Soviets, and as failing to pursue a policy of vigorous negotiation at the bargaining table. In American eyes, unilateral disarmament surrenders everything without negotiation.

Harris surveys find that nearly eight out of ten Americans (78 percent) oppose the dismantling of the U.S. nuclear arsenal before other countries have agreed to do the same.[1] Other survey findings on unilateral disarmament have similar results.

Traditional Arms Control

The arms control framework favored by five administrations before the Reagan Administration typifies policies that have inconsistent political support. The concept of arms control gets widespread endorsement when it is stated as an abstract goal. Three out of four Americans favor "the U.S. signing another arms agreement with the Soviet Union to limit nuclear weapons on both sides."[2] Americans are virtually unanimous (89 percent) that worldwide arms control should be an important goal of U.S. foreign policy (see Chart 21).

Support for arms control in the abstract, however, does not translate into automatic approval of arms control agreements. In 1985, for example, the Soviets announced a unilateral ban on testing of nuclear weapons and invited the United States to join in negotiations for a complete ban. The *Los Angeles Times* found that the public was divided equally about the wisdom of joining such a moratorium.[3] When opinion poll questions about arms control agreements draw atten-

---

21 **Support for the Idea of Arms Control**

Q. Please say whether you think [arms control] should be a very important foreign policy goal, a somewhat important goal, or not an important goal at all.

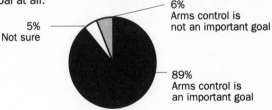

6%
Arms control is
not an important goal

5%
Not sure

89%
Arms control is
an important goal

Source: Gallup, for the Chicago Council on Foreign Relations. November 1985.

tion to their drawbacks, the public's reservations are triggered, and agreements lose much of their appeal.

The reason for this is that most arms control agreements
match some of the public's values but violate others. On the
positive side, arms control is seen as a way of alleviating world
tensions and reducing the threat of nuclear war. It also opens
up channels of negotiation with the Soviets. It therefore
scores well on these two values. On the negative side, it is
seen by most Americans as *weakening* our military strength.
There is a widespread feeling that U.S. negotiators do not
always protect American interests. Only a small fraction of
the public (17 percent) has a "great deal of confidence" that
our negotiators "will protect U.S. interests and that they will
not make agreements that might endanger American security."[4]

For most Americans the biggest drawback to arms control
is that it appears to rely on the good will of the Soviets. A
majority (55 percent) believe the Soviet Union cannot be
trusted to keep their part of a bargain on nuclear arms control (76 percent think that the United States *can* be trusted)
(see Chart 22). When the issue of trust is raised, support for
arms control evaporates rapidly. The nonpartisan Public
Agenda Foundation found that when people consider the
need to trust the Soviet Union, they are hesitant to support
any arms control proposals. Nearly half of the population (45
percent) endorses the statement that "because the Soviets will
not keep their end of the bargain, we should not sign any
agreements limiting arms."[5]

In sum, the arms control approach of the past few decades
clearly fails two of the four tests of public acceptability: it
scores well on reduced vulnerability and negotiations, but it
does poorly on military strength and mistrust.

Can be trusted:

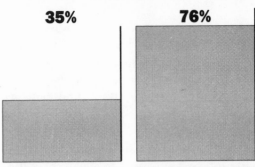

35%	76%

If the U.S. and the Soviet Union were to reach an agreement on nuclear weapons control, do you think the Russians could be trusted to keep their part of the bargain, or not?*

Do you think the United States can or cannot be trusted to keep its part of the agreements in the INF (missile) treaty?*

*Survey conducted among registered voters.
Source: Market Opinion Research, for the Americans Talk Security Project, 1988.

The Nuclear Freeze

In the early 1980s the prospect of a mutually verifiable nuclear freeze excited a great deal of attention. At its peak the freeze commanded impressive public support:

- Eighty-three percent of Americans said they would favor a "freeze on the production of nuclear weapons in both the U.S. and the Soviet Union."
- Eighty-one percent said they would favor a congressional resolution calling for the United States to negotiate a verifiable freeze agreement with the Soviet

Union, under which both sides would ban the future production, storage, and use of their nuclear weapons (see Chart 23).

Such opinion polls encouraged peace movement leaders to believe that they had found an approach to the arms race with real political punch. Prior to Mr. Reagan's re-election in 1984, freeze proponents were certain they had a winning issue in their hands. Tirelessly they cited evidence showing that a mutually verifiable freeze enjoyed very high levels of public support.

But these poll responses did not mean what freeze movement activists interpreted them to mean. Freeze supporters interpreted the findings as an indication of firm support for a *policy* of freezing weapons development on both sides. Interviews showed, however, that this literal interpretation was incorrect. For most Americans, supporting the freeze was an emotional reaction to the folly of "overkill" — the idea that

23 Support for the Idea of a Nuclear Freeze

Favor freeze:

83%

Would you favor or oppose a freeze on the production of nuclear weapons both in the U.S. and the Soviet Union?

81%

Would you favor or oppose Congress passing a resolution that would call upon the U.S. to negotiate a nuclear freeze agreement with the Soviet Union under which both sides would ban future production, storage, and the use of their weapons?

Sources: NBC News/Associated Press, 1982; Harris, for *Business Week*, 1983.

both sides have enough weapons to destroy each other many times over. The image of a freeze proved to be a symbolic way of saying "Enough is enough; there must be some alternative to this madness."

An intriguing set of questions asked by the Roper Organization illustrates how the freeze fails to match some of the public's criteria.[6] Roper found that most Americans see the freeze as a concrete step toward reducing tensions and making the world safer. The most convincing argument for the freeze (other than the fact that it will save money) is that it will reduce tensions and avoid the threat of war. Nearly six out of ten of those polled (58 percent) found this argument at least somewhat convincing. None of the other arguments for the freeze was as convincing.

The freeze got mixed scores on another value — encouraging negotiations. The public was divided as to whether it would or would not improve the climate for negotiations. (Only 36 percent thought that it would encourage the Soviets to follow up with further arms reductions.) The public was also split (46 percent to 42 percent) on whether a freeze would remove incentives for further arms negotiations.

The main source of support for the freeze comes from the belief that we and the Soviets already have enough weapons to destroy each other many times over (90 percent) — an emotional protest to "the nuclear madness." The biggest problem with the freeze, from the public's perspective, is that (as with arms control) it involves trusting the Soviet Union. Two thirds of the public (66 percent) believe the Soviets cannot be trusted to live up to the terms of a nuclear freeze agreement. There is also widespread public concern that a freeze would lock the United States into a weaker military position and prevent America from modernizing its weapons systems (see Chart 24).

Thus, like arms control, the freeze scores badly on two of the public's criteria — mistrust of the Soviets and preservation of U.S. military strength. From the public's perspective, the freeze is only slightly different from traditional arms control. Both are seen as reducing tensions and the immediate chance of nuclear war. But both also arouse deeply held fears.

Détente

Recently there has been some public discussion about reviving the détente policy of the 1970s. The rationale is, first, that the Gorbachev government may be more flexible than earlier Soviet leaderships, and second, that the Soviet economy is weaker than it was in the seventies. If the oil glut continues, the Soviet Union, one of the largest oil producers in the world, will find itself even more susceptible to economic pressure, because it will have an even greater need for Western technology than in the past.

24 Reservations About a Nuclear Freeze

Q. Here are some arguments that have been made against an immediate nuclear freeze. For an argument to be convincing, it has to be both important and true. Would you tell me . . . whether you find [the following] a convincing or not a convincing argument against an immediate freeze: "A freeze would prevent the U.S. from modernizing its aging weapons and introduce more reliable, less vulnerable nuclear weapons systems."

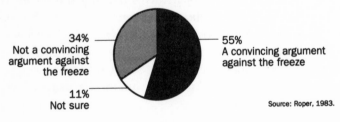

34%
Not a convincing
argument against
the freeze

55%
A convincing argument
against the freeze

11%
Not sure

Source: Roper, 1983.

Our analysis of public opinion suggests that détente would meet the same fate as the freeze and traditional arms control, for the same reasons. Détente wins high marks as an abstract theory. The word *détente* literally means "relaxation of tension," and most Americans welcome this in dealings with the Soviets, particularly on nuclear arms. But support for a renewed détente policy, in the 1970s style, would be unstable and inconsistent.

Détente has had an up-and-down history with the public. In the mid-seventies it was a popular policy, as we have pointed out, but the public soured on it after the invasion of Afghanistan. Recently its stock has rebounded. Almost two thirds of the public say that they prefer détente to a Cold War policy; only 33 percent say that they wish to deal with the USSR as a potential enemy (see Chart 25).

The pattern of public support for détente is similar to that for arms control and the freeze. On the plus side, the policy is seen as reducing tensions and encouraging negotiations; on the minus side, it shares the weaknesses of the other two approaches. A majority of Americans (68 percent) believe that "the Soviets used détente as an opportunity to build up their armed forces while lulling us into a false sense of security."[7] Détente involves trusting the Soviets and, people believe, tempts the United States to reduce its military strength.

The Strategic Defense Initiative (SDI)

Mr. Reagan's conservatism offered the public a very different set of policies, the centerpiece of which is the Strategic Defense Initiative (SDI), popularly known as Star Wars.

In some respects SDI is a research program, not a policy. It has been presented to the public as a program that does not rely on negotiations or on Soviet good faith. Essentially,

1980   1987

Q. The U.S. has had two different policies in dealing with the Soviet Union. One, called détente, was based on cooperation and trading with them as a friendly nation. The other, called the Cold War, was based on dealing with them as a potential enemy. Once the situation in Afghanistan is settled, which do you think would be the best course for the U.S. to follow in dealing with the Soviet Union—a policy of détente or the policy of Cold War?*

Q. What do you think the United States should do now—should the United States try harder to reduce tensions with the Russians, or should the United States get tougher in its dealings with the Russsians?*

Détente: *Try harder:*

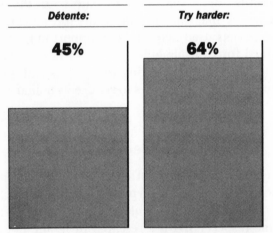

45%   **64%**

*1980 sample drawn from registered voters; 1987 survey conducted among American voters.
Sources: Yankelovich, Skelly and White for *Time*, January 1980;
Marttila & Kiley, Inc., for the Americans Talk Security Project, October 1987.

the Strategic Defense Initiative is a unilateral way of increasing U.S. military preparedness. Indeed, moving ahead with SDI may involve compromising the antiballistic missile treaty of 1972, which many believe to be the single most valuable achievement of the long and arduous arms control process.

SDI supporters have been encouraged by high levels of public endorsement in the opinion polls. A look at the polls, however, shows that this policy suffers from as much volatility as the other policies we have discussed — although the reasons are different.

Like the other policies, SDI wins high marks when presented abstractly. Most Americans believe it is a good idea. A clear majority of the public favor plans to develop SDI (see Chart 26). Most Americans are actually surprised to learn that we do not have a system of this kind in place today. Two thirds say that they are *not* aware that the United States now has no means of defending itself from incoming ballistic missiles. An even higher proportion (83 percent) say they are not aware that "the U.S. has a treaty with the Soviet Union not to protect Americans from a Soviet missile attack" (see Chart 27).

---

26 **Support for the Idea of SDI**

Q. Next, I want to ask you about the Strategic Defense Initiative, the program known as Star Wars. Do you approve or disapprove of the continued development of Star Wars?*

11%
Not sure

54%
Approve

34%
Disapprove

*Survey conducted among American voters.
Source: Marttila & Kiley, Inc., for the Americans Talk Security Project, October 1987.

SDI scores best on the values for which the other policies do worst. It is seen as enhancing U.S. military strength, and it does not rely on the good will of the Soviet Union. Though many of its critics stress its technological unworkability, the public is not impressed with this argument. Six out of ten Americans believe that SDI could be made to work, and belief in its workability is highest among those who say they know most about it.[8]

But overall, support for SDI is unstable — almost as unstable as support for the freeze. The main problem with SDI is that overwhelming majorities believe that it will escalate the arms race. For example,

- seventy-five percent believe that "once it looked as though the U.S. was capable of defending against today's nuclear weapons, the Soviets would then go all-out to develop new kinds of nuclear and other weapons we couldn't defend against."[9]
- seventy-five percent believe that "if we build the Star

27 Public Misperceptions About U.S. Missile Defense Systems

Q. Are you aware that the U.S. now has no means of defending itself from incoming ballistic missiles?

68%
Not aware that
no system exists

Q. Did you know that the U.S. has a treaty with the Soviet Union not to protect Americans from a Soviet missile attack?

83%
Do not know
about this treaty

Sources: Sindlinger, 1982; Finkelstein, 1985.

Wars system, the Soviets will just start building more and more weapons until they can penetrate it" (see Chart 28).

The high cost of SDI is also a public concern. Sixty-nine percent feel that even if it is a good idea, developing a Star Wars system is too costly, especially when "our federal deficit is already at an all-time high" (see Chart 29). And although the American people do support SDI as a concept, they clearly do not support it as an alternative to negotiations with the Soviets. Most people believe that if we have a choice between pushing ahead with SDI and reaching an arms agreement, we should abandon SDI. By a three-to-one majority (74 percent to 20 percent), Americans think that reaching arms reduction agreements is a more important goal than developing space weapons. There is strong support (59 percent) for a treaty that will prevent both countries from using weapons in outer space (see Chart 30 on next page).

One way to understand the findings on SDI is to separate the policy's technical and political components. Most of the

28 **SDI and the Arms Race**

Q. If we build a Star Wars system, the Soviets will just start building more and better nuclear weapons until they can penetrate it.*

6%
Not sure

19%
Disagree

75%
Agree

*Survey conducted among American voters.
Source: Marttila & Kiley, Inc., for the Americans Talk Security Project, October 1987.

29 The Cost of SDI

Q. Even if it's a good idea, Star Wars costs too much to build and deploy, especially at a time when our federal deficit is already at an all-time high.*

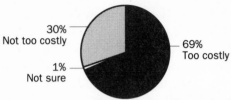

30%
Not too costly

1%
Not sure

69%
Too costly

*Survey conducted among registered voters.
Source: The Daniel Yankelovich Group, Inc., for the Americans Talk Security Project, 1988.

30 Greater Importance of Arms Reduction than SDI

Q. In general, which would you say is more important: for the U.S. to develop space-based weapons to defend against nuclear attack, or for the U.S. and the Soviet Union to agree to a substantial reduction of nuclear arms by both countries?

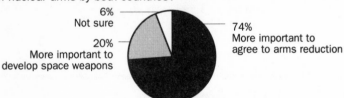

6%
Not sure

20%
More important to
develop space weapons

74%
More important to
agree to arms reduction

Q. It has been proposed that the U.S. and the Soviet Union agree to outlaw the use of all military weapons in outer space. Generally speaking, do you favor or oppose such an agreement?

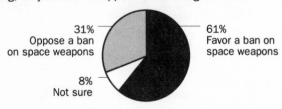

31%
Oppose a ban
on space weapons

8%
Not sure

61%
Favor a ban on
space weapons

Sources: ABC News/*Washington Post*, October 1985; *Los Angeles Times*, November 1985.

support for SDI is as an alternative to the horrors of MAD; the will to defend ourselves against attack seems less blood-thirsty than a threat of revenge. Clearly the idea of using technology for defense rather than offense has captured people's imaginations. But the public rejects SDI as a political program to expand the arms race and by-pass negotiations. There may be more durable support for such technical systems within the context of a different approach to a cooperative defense strategy, as we discuss in Chapter 7.

Favorable public response to SDI is based mainly on the idea that it is designed to protect population centers. The concept of a shield or umbrella placed over our cities holds a

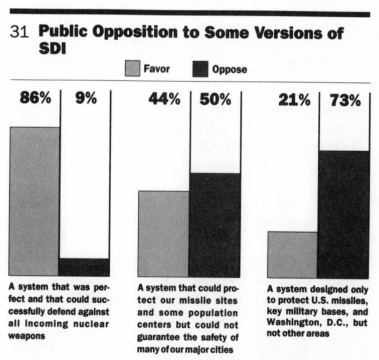

31 Public Opposition to Some Versions of SDI

☐ Favor   ■ Oppose

| 86% | 9% | 44% | 50% | 21% | 73% |

A system that was perfect and that could successfully defend against all incoming nuclear weapons

A system that could protect our missile sites and some population centers but could not guarantee the safety of many of our major cities

A system designed only to protect U.S. missiles, key military bases, and Washington, D.C., but not other areas

Source: Marttila & Kiley, Inc., for The Women's Action for Nuclear Disarmament Education Fund, 1985.

powerful emotional appeal for Americans, especially since it promises to restore the invulnerability the United States once enjoyed. Critics of SDI argue, however, that since it is technically impossible for the system to protect civilian populations, its real purpose is to protect military targets such as ground-based missile systems. But public support for SDI evaporates when the system is seen as a protection for military targets only (see Chart 31).

It is illuminating to compare these five policies. With the exception of unilateral disarmament, all match some of the public's values but not others. There is a close relationship among three policies — arms control, the nuclear freeze, and détente. All three are seen as reducing one of the two major threats that concern the public — the threat of nuclear war. But none of them deals convincingly with the other threat — the concern for Soviet power and expansionism. SDI, in con-

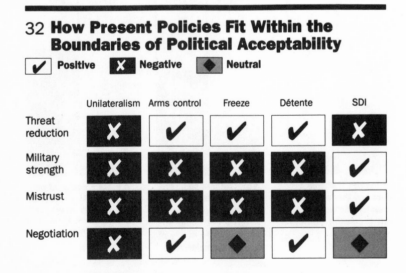

32 How Present Policies Fit Within the Boundaries of Political Acceptability

✔ Positive	✘ Negative	◆ Neutral

	Unilateralism	Arms control	Freeze	Détente	SDI
Threat reduction	✘	✔	✔	✔	✘
Military strength	✘	✘	✘	✘	✔
Mistrust	✘	✘	✘	✘	✔
Negotiation	✘	✔	◆	✔	◆

trast, has the opposite pattern of strengths and weaknesses. It is seen as a way of increasing American military strength and putting a check on Soviet power and expansionism, but by increasing the risk of nuclear war. For a summary assessment, see Chart 32.

Public Judgment
of the Reagan Doctrine

SINCE SDI IS MERELY one part of an overall policy that has come to be known as the Reagan Doctrine, we now want to see how this doctrine as a whole is assessed by the public. In a narrow sense, the term refers to the policy of supporting "freedom fighters" who oppose Marxist-Leninist regimes in Third World countries: armed forces such as the contras in Nicaragua and the Mujaheddin rebels in Afghanistan. In a broader sense, the Reagan Doctrine refers to the full range of Reagan policies in their competitive stance toward the Soviet Union.

In this sense, the doctrine has evolved considerably from Mr. Reagan's first term. It did *not*, it should be noted, start with the people. Mr. Reagan forged his hard-line ideas about communism, the Soviet Union, and how to deal with the Soviet leaders out of his personal experience in combating communist influence in the Screen Actors' Guild. He correctly assumed that he had a public mandate to put his convictions into practice. In his second term, however, taking the changing public mood into account, Mr. Reagan began to modify his strategy. He moderated his rhetoric, moving away from his characterization of the Soviet Union as an "evil empire," and he began to encourage negotiations and summit meetings. In 1985, at the Geneva summit, he endorsed the concept of common security. In 1986, at Reykjavik, he proposed the total elimination of nuclear arms and delivery systems, moving far beyond the desires of the U.S. military command, our European allies, the mainstream of his party, and even the Democratic opposition. In 1987 he pushed forward serious negotiations with the Soviets on an intermediate nuclear forces (INF) arms reduction treaty.

With so many changes, the Reagan Doctrine has found itself beset with internal tensions. Part of the difficulty comes from the conflicting pulls of Mr. Reagan's conservative ideology and the pragmatism of the public, but disagreement between the conservative and moderate elements in the Reagan Administration has generated most of it. Fierce struggles occur between those who want to deal with the Soviets and those who do not; those who insist that the United States should regain military superiority and those who are ready to accept parity; those who favor arms control and those who do not; those who wish to destabilize the Soviets and those who accept their legitimacy; those who court every chance to weaken the Soviets and those who are more aversive to risk.

In this chapter we analyze the fit between public values and the conservative version of the Reagan Doctrine. Logically, that version is more internally consistent than the moderate version. Politically, it offers the American public a clear-cut choice. And psychologically, Americans find it useful to confront this choice head-on: it is part of the hard work needed to adapt our thinking to the nuclear age.

Priorities of the Reagan Doctrine

The conservative Reagan Doctrine has one foot in the nuclear age and the other in the prenuclear world. It recognizes
the no-win nature of nuclear war, but it also continues to
fight the threat of Soviet expansion with every available weapon, including nuclear arms.

Under the Reagan Doctrine our national priority has been
to counter Soviet expansionism at all costs and to accept the
risks this entails. The editor of *Commentary*, Norman Podhoretz, an important conservative spokesman, defends this priority with a clear understanding of its consequences:

> In advocating an anti-Communist strategy of containment, am I
> calling for an eternity of confrontation and the risk of war with-
> out letup, without surcease, and without any hope of victory at
> the end? It would be dishonest to deny . . . that this might indeed
> be the prospect. It is a horrifying prospect from which one's first
> impulse is to shrink. But the prospect from the other side is more
> horrifying still: a universal Gulag and a life that is otherwise
> nasty, brutish and short.[1]

These few sentences make explicit some of the assumptions
of Reagan conservatism. An anticommunist strategy is assumed to require confrontation and "the risk of war without
letup." Soviet expansionism is seen as leading to a "universal
Gulag" that could ultimately deprive America of its liberty.
This prospect is "more horrifying" than the danger of nuclear war and should therefore take precedence over it.

Millions of Americans share Mr. Podhoretz's dark suspi-
cion of the Soviets. To protect American freedom, they are
willing to risk death itself. But when pressed, the majority of
the people refuse to follow Podhoretz's logic. Most Americans do *not* accept the inevitability of "an eternity of confrontation" and the grim, unrelieved threat of a no-win, no-

survivor nuclear war. They do *not* place the Soviet threat above the threat of nuclear war. And they do *not* believe that countering it must involve keeping the risk of war at a maximum pitch of intensity.

Survey findings show that the public does regard Soviet expansion as a major threat. Nearly six out of ten Americans say that "Soviet aggression around the world" is a serious threat to our national security. About the same number also cite the buildup of nuclear weapons on both sides as a serious threat. Both threats receive equal credence (see Chart 33).

The Reagan Doctrine holds that the United States should be prepared at all times to take full advantage of Soviet weaknesses. This approach mirrors the Soviets' past tactics in their relations with the United States. In the ebb and flow of events, there are times when America finds itself in the ascendancy in world influence and other times when its influence recedes. The middle and late 1970s were a time of relative weakness for America. The United States had suffered an

33 The Threats of Soviet Expansion and the Nuclear Arms Buildup

Agree:

59%

Soviet aggression around the world is a serious threat to our national security.*

64%

The buildup of nuclear weapons on both sides is a serious threat to our national security.*

*Survey conducted among registered voters.
Source: The Daniel Yankelovich Group, Inc., for the Americans Talk Security Project, 1988.

unprecedented military defeat in Southeast Asia. American political will was reluctant to engage the Soviets aggressively elsewhere in the Third World (for example, in Angola). There was a public backlash against the military, and defense budgets were cut in favor of social programs. The Soviets concluded that the so-called correlation of forces — military power, economic power, political will — had shifted against America.

As Americans are well aware, the Soviets were aggressive in exploiting this trend. By the mid-1980s, however, the correlation of forces had shifted back in favor of the United States, and the Reagan Doctrine was determined to take advantage of it.

One difficulty with the strategy of relentlessly exploiting the adversary's weaknesses is that the United States and the Soviet Union will invariably be out of sync with each other. Whichever country has the momentary advantage will use it, yielding to the temptation to treat the other in a humiliating fashion. The bitter result is a cycle of action and reaction, a heritage of resentment, a determination to humiliate the other side when our turn comes around again. If the history of the arms race teaches us anything, it is that whenever one country takes advantage of the momentary weakness of the other, the result is an escalation that weakens the security of *both* countries.

Strikingly, there is little public support for weakening the Soviets when they are vulnerable. The majority of Americans are concerned that such a strategy will backfire. Nearly two thirds (63 percent) endorse the view that "the U.S. should not weaken the Soviets at every opportunity because if we weaken them too much, they may become more dangerous" (see Chart 34). A majority oppose the tactic of risking nuclear war to weaken the Soviet economy or military power (see Chart 35).

34 Public Views on Weakening the Soviets

Q. Do you agree or disagree with the following statement? "The U.S. should not weaken the Soviets at every opportunity because if we weaken them too much, they may become more dangerous, like cornered rats."

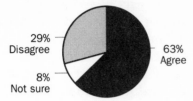

29%
Disagree

8%
Not sure

63%
Agree

Source: The Public Agenda Foundation, 1984.

35 Public Views on Undermining the Soviet Economy

Q. Many Americans differ on the best way to deal with the Soviet Union. For example, our political leaders believe that it's no use trying to negotiate or make deals with the Soviets. They say that we have to weaken the Soviet economy and their military power even at the risk of nuclear war. Do you agree with this statement completely, somewhat, or not at all?

5%
Not sure

6%
Completely
agree

35%
Somewhat
agree

54%
Disagree

Source: Yankelovich, Skelly and White, for *Time*, November 1985.

A closely related priority of Reagan conservatism is the determination to regain military superiority. In seeking to recoup a military edge through SDI, the United States is in effect reviving its reliance on nuclear diplomacy. But even if we were to win a few years of technological advantage in space, it is doubtful that the edge would last for long. The Soviets have several options. They can seek to close the gap through their own research and development. They can acquire the new technology in indirect ways, through other countries. They can steal it. Most ominous, they can overwhelm or by-pass new U.S. defensive systems by building up their ground-based ballistic missiles and MIRVing them more extensively, and/or they can strengthen their arsenal of cruise missiles. This is what Mr. Gorbachev has threatened to do, both in private and in public.

If past performance is a guide, the Soviets will keep their word. In the 1970s they made immense sacrifices to achieve military parity with the West. Security-conscious to the point of paranoia, they have proved willing to make greater sacrifices than America and its allies do, particularly in maintaining a large and well-trained army. Again and again they have proved capable of catching up with America's most important technological innovations, usually within a brief, three- to five-year span.[2] And so an unending competition for nuclear superiority would drive the arms race to yet another stage, accelerating humanity's move toward the nuclear abyss.

Even if the United States could develop a margin of superiority, it would remain vulnerable. Robert McNamara points out that at the time of the Cuban missile crisis in 1962, overwhelming nuclear superiority gave America no real security from attack from the Soviets' limited nuclear arsenal. The premise that nuclear superiority equals security relies heavily on Soviet prudence and rationality; it does not take into account a Soviet (or American) miscalculation or a burst of irrational anger that could unleash a nuclear holocaust even in the face of decisive superiority.[3] Who can guarantee that another Stalin — secretive, isolated, paranoic, barbaric, and ultimately suicidal — will not take power? Who would want to make American — and world — survival dependent on the Soviets' prudence and rationality? What conceivable value could a few extra nuclear bombs have in such circumstances?

The heart of the Reagan Doctrine is a commitment to support rebellion against communist governments anywhere in the world in the name of the universal right of freedom. In Mr. Reagan's words, "Our mission is to nourish and defend freedom and democracy . . . we must not break faith with those who are risking their lives on every continent, from Afghanistan to Nicaragua, to defy Soviet-supported aggression and secure rights which have been ours from birth."

The Reagan Administration's support of counterinsurgencies has concentrated mostly on Marxist governments that became Soviet outposts in the 1970s. But in principle, since freedom is a universal right, the Reagan Doctrine promises U.S. government support for freedom fighters everywhere. The Reagan Doctrine is the counterpart to the Soviet commitment to support wars of national liberation everywhere, which Khrushchev deemed a sacred obligation of the socialist motherland. The support of freedom as a universal right is sacred in the American credo. A series of collisions between two such "sacred" doctrines could readily escalate into a quasi religious war in which pragmatic compromise would be regarded as immoral, if not evil.

The Reagan Doctrine lacks any room for agreement with the Soviets on how to keep the U.S.-USSR rivalry in Third World countries from leading to confrontation. Therefore, the dangers of that rivalry are likely to grow, and in the long run lead to nuclear confrontation.

Perhaps the most distinctive priority of the conservative Reagan Doctrine is the desire to be independent of negotiations with the Soviets — to "go it alone." Mr. Reagan has criticized the arms control agreements reached by Richard Nixon when he was president, and has even questioned Nixon's conservative credentials. The Reagan Doctrine assumes (correctly) that the Soviets will concur only with agreements that grant them full military parity with the West, and it is precisely this status that conservatives are unwilling to concede. They believe it is wrong to make American security hostage to a Soviet *nyet*. In this view, America should seek to build a position of superior strength which the Soviets have no choice but to accept.

Adherents of the Reagan Doctrine believe that such a condition is the only policy that can truly safeguard America's freedom. If America is to prevail, it must pursue a go-it-alone approach. The Reagan Doctrine criticizes past policies for giving the United States the worst of both worlds: arms control agreements that constrain the United States without yielding the one reward that would make military parity acceptable—a genuine increase in U.S. security as a result of stopping the arms race.

Acceptability to the Public

It is illuminating to discuss the Reagan Doctrine from the perspective of the four values the public wants U.S. policy to embody. The doctrine is responsive to two of the public's demands: it does not depend on a naive trust of the Soviets, and it does emphasize American military strength. Reagan conservatism is strongest in precisely the areas where policy alternatives are politically weakest. But it violates the public's other two criteria.

The doctrine's go-it-alone aspects clearly fail to meet the public's demand for negotiations in good faith. Widespread agreement with the Soviets is possible only if conservatives abandon their requirement that America regain a military edge. It is almost inconceivable that the Soviets will give up their hard-won military parity for the sake of reaching an arms agreement with the United States. To do so would spell certain trouble for Mr. Gorbachev among his conservative colleagues. And any major arms agreement based on the principle of military parity will be resisted by American conservatives, even if it is packaged to be palatable to them. In their eyes, such an agreement would no longer be faithful to the Reagan Doctrine. Therefore, if a far-reaching arms reduction accord is reached with the Soviets, the conservative wing of the Reagan constituency will feel betrayed.

Finally, and most important, the conservative Reagan Doctrine fails to meet the majority's demand that the threat of nuclear war be reduced. The Reagan Doctrine accepts the risks of accelerating the nuclear arms race to deter Soviet expansion, but this position is rejected by the mainstream of the electorate.

In seeking to keep the Soviets off balance and to win the arms race, the Reagan Doctrine makes good sense to that minority of Americans who are convinced that we are locked in a life-or-death struggle with communism and who accept the dangers of nuclear confrontation because they believe it to be inevitable anyway. These are the convictions of perhaps one quarter of the electorate. Supporters of the Reagan Doctrine have used marketing skills in packaging their ideology so that it appears to have a broader appeal. As we have seen, the result is a thin layer of surface support resting on a thick layer of latent public dissatisfaction.

Primal Fears

We must always keep in mind that underlying every individual's values are primal fears, the most profound roots of human behavior. Two different definitions of *primal* are involved. The fear of nuclear war is primal in that it involves a biological fear that human survival will be threatened. It is true that some American fundamentalists are fatalistic about a nuclear apocalypse, and even welcome it as the fulfillment of a Biblical prediction (the Book of Daniel). But the majority of Americans are convinced that the nuclear threat is controllable. They are prepared to spend any amount of money (hence their support for SDI) and make any other sacrifice to keep the danger at bay.

The fear of Soviet expansionism is also primal, not in a biological sense but in a cultural sense. Human culture revolves around patterns of shared meanings and values. Americans see Soviet expansionism as a threat to their most fundamental values: freedom, family, religious faith, democracy, control over one's destiny, and all of the other things that give American life its meaning. These values are nearly as basic as the survival instinct. Those Americans who support the Reagan Doctrine do so because they believe it protects American values at all costs.

Where the majority of the American people part company with the Reagan Doctrine is over the priority assigned to the two threats. In the public mind, the threat of Soviet expansionism is not more dangerous than the threat of nuclear war. The electorate is pragmatic, more eager to negotiate constraints on our competition with the Soviets than to flirt with confrontation. Nearly six Americans out of ten (59 percent) believe that the United States would be safer if we "stopped treating the Soviets as enemies and tried to hammer out our differences in a live-and-let-live spirit." This view is even more widespread among younger Americans: it is endorsed by 69 percent of those under thirty years of age (see Chart 36).

The conservative architects of the Reagan Doctrine reject this majority view in favor of the opposite conclusion. From their own analysis, they have assessed the risk of nuclear war as slight and the risk of Soviet expansionism as great. They therefore conclude that it is worth accepting the risk of nuclear war to block the greater threat. But this conclusion is not out in the open where the voters can perceive it and respond to it. Because it is hidden from the public view, the American people are deceived about it and confused about what to believe.

Our conclusion is that in any serious and sustained public debate, a significant minority will continue to embrace the conservative version of the Reagan Doctrine, while the majority will opt for a credible alternative if one is presented to them.

36 Public Views on Treating the Soviets as Enemies

Q. If we stopped treating the Soviets as enemies and tried to hammer out our differences in a live-and-let-live spirit, would [it] make the U.S. safer, less safe, or wouldn't it make any difference?

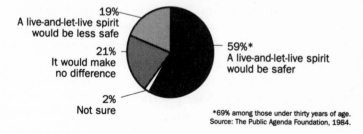

19%
A live-and-let-live spirit would be less safe

21%
It would make no difference

2%
Not sure

59%*
A live-and-let-live spirit would be safer

*69% among those under thirty years of age.
Source: The Public Agenda Foundation, 1984.

New Realities

THE PRECEDING CHAPTERS are concerned with identifying public values, evaluating the experts' policies in terms of these values, and specifying how and why the policies fall short. Our thesis is that only when the people are able to compare the experts' proposals with an alternative that is built on public values can they come to the kind of public judgment that an enduring consensus demands. In earlier times—before World War II, for example—political and military crises perpetrated by totalitarian dictators led to a mobilization of both public opinion and political leadership. But these are not such times.

Implicit in starting with the people is the premise that values and goals must be considered prior to expert knowledge. The goals shape the policy. If we put the threat of nuclear war ahead of the threat of Soviet expansionism, we end up with one type of policy (for example, the policies favored by the peace movement). If we put the threat of Soviet expansionism above all else, including survival itself, we get a different policy (for example, the Reagan Doctrine). If we give both threats equal weight, as the public demands, the resulting policy will differ sharply from the other two, as we shall see below.

Thus far we have described public values regarding U.S.-Soviet relations in two ways: as demands that American policy give equal weight to both of the public's primal fears (the threat of nuclear war and the threat to American liberty), and as a set of boundary lines within which policies must fit. These descriptions are interchangeable. The four criteria of public acceptability are simply a concrete way of expressing the public's fears and convictions: Americans believe that reducing the threat of nuclear war must be pursued through good-faith negotiations with the Soviets, and they also believe that the United States can hold Soviet ambitions in check only by keeping America strong militarily and by avoiding excessive trust in the Russians.

In formulating a "people's option" — a policy that starts with public values — we must avoid the mistake we have accused the experts of making. The experts, we have said, have erred in ignoring the public; they turn a deaf ear to public values. We must not now turn a deaf ear to the experts and their information. Starting with the people's values is not a simple matter of inferring foreign policy from public opinion. The experts' special knowledge must be factored in.

Starting with the public's fears and keeping in mind the boundaries of public acceptability, we must take into account the new realities to which the country's policies must adapt. The world has changed drastically since the containment/deterrence policy was initiated. Unless we reckon with these changes, we risk shaping a policy that meets public values but is unrealistic.

In the following sections we summarize some of the most

important new geopolitical realities that have rendered America's old policies obsolete. These include

- the Soviet achievement of nuclear parity ("parity shock");
- a change in the locus and nature of the Soviet threat, from Western Europe to the Third World and from a political challenge to a military one;
- a worldwide surge of nationalism;
- the failure of Marxist-Leninist command economies to create the kind of growth and economic development most nations want;
- changes in Soviet attitudes and policies introduced by Secretary-General Gorbachev; and
- the need to make a better transition from zero-sum security to the principle of common security.

Parity Shock

The United States and the USSR presently pursue their own policies without much understanding of their impact on each other. Both sides are motivated by domestic concerns and by their conception of strategic superiority. It is in this context that we must grasp the full meaning of "parity shock."

Parity shock means absorbing the fact that the United States has lost whatever protection was afforded by nuclear superiority and now exists in a balance of terror in which the nuclear forces on both sides have passed a critical threshold: each nation can at will destroy the other. This is the threat that intolerably diminishes U.S. (and Soviet) national security. The fact of absolute mutual vulnerability does not require parity in the sense of equality in numbers of weapons. It does require an invulnerable second-strike capability. It is in this sense that the Soviet achievement is a source of parity shock.

It has become a truism that survival in the nuclear age requires changed patterns of human behavior. In prenuclear times war was sometimes regarded as "the continuation of diplomacy by other means." In the wars of the past there were winners, spoils, territory, new beginnings — perhaps even valor and glory and honor. But in nuclear war there are no winners, there is no glory and honor. There is only tragedy and death, not only for the combatants but also for humanity and perhaps for all earthly forms of life.

As we have seen, consciousness of this fact has grown steadily. Virtually all Americans now understand how devastating the threat of nuclear war is. Yet this consciousness, though broadly based, remains shallow. It has not yet transformed behavior or policy. Parity shock means bringing to public consciousness the full significance of the nuclear age, which Americans were not obliged to confront as long as the United States had an edge. With parity, nuclear confrontation truly becomes unthinkable, and the nation must begin to recognize that there is no security in a nuclear arms race that neither side can permit the other to win.

Changes in the Nature of the Soviet Threat

In the early postwar period, the authors of the containment policy visualized the Soviet threat in the form of Soviet troops and tanks sweeping across Western Europe while local communist parties exploited economic disarray and political unrest to weaken these countries, making them ripe for communist revolution.

After Korea, Cuba, Vietnam, four Middle Eastern wars, Angola, Ethiopia, El Salvador, and Nicaragua, it is clear that

Soviet efforts to destabilize Western Europe are not the major threat. Eurocommunism, which seemed so robust until the 1970s, has virtually disappeared. The Italian communist party, the largest in Europe, is almost indistinguishable from traditional European social democratic parties. In the mid-1980s the Mitterrand government in France drastically reduced the influence of the French communist party. Any thought the Soviets might now entertain of invading Western Europe is checked by the fragility of the Soviet relationship with the Warsaw Pact nations. The Soviets are having enough trouble controlling their Eastern European empire without launching military adventures that would oblige them to count on the loyalty of the Poles, the Czechs, and the Hungarians. They would not relish the prospect of having their Eastern European allies at their backs.

Moreover, the Soviets do not like huge risks, especially if safe strategies are available. Thus far they have not had great success in separating the United States from its Western European allies. There is some tension in the Atlantic alliance, and much can be done to strengthen the bonds. But Western Europe is not where the Soviet threat appears to reside.

The threat comes mainly from Soviet involvement in the Third World. The major wars in Korea and Vietnam both lost American lives and had an enormous impact on our domestic politics. The Soviet threat in Central America can readily affect the global balance of power. If Cuba and Nicaragua, backed by Moscow, can extend armed insurgency in Central America, the security of the United States will be weakened both directly and indirectly. The direct threat is to Panama and U.S. shipping, and ultimately to Mexico. The indirect threat, as the Bipartisan Commission on Latin America makes clear, deflects major resources away from Europe and Asia, reducing U.S. influence elsewhere (we would be perceived as unable to influence events in our own back yard) and causing even greater violence and misery in the region.

A serious threat to Pakistan, Saudi Arabia, or Iran could damage U.S. interests in the Persian Gulf. A communist threat to the Philippines could jeopardize our ties with our allies in Southeast Asia. Both liberals and conservatives have argued that since U.S. interests are global and the world grows ever more interdependent, the loss of any country to Marxism-Leninism counts as a loss for the United States and a threat to the national security. But even the most hardened cold warrior will admit some exceptions. For example, the Marxist-Leninist regimes of Benin in West Africa and the Democratic Republic of the Congo in Central Africa do not rank as high risks even among our most ideologically conservative policy makers. But a number of strategically located countries in various other places have emerged since 1975 as Marxist-Leninist governments. These governments are dependent on Moscow for their continued existence and in turn extend the Soviet Union's global military reach.

The Powerful Impact of Nationalism

Just as the Soviet threat has shifted, so too have the limiting factors on Soviet expansionism. More than forty years of post–World War II experience have taught the world that the major force blocking the spread of Soviet influence is not U.S. arms but nationalism. When the United Nations was founded in 1945, it had 50 nations as members; now it has 159. The postwar period has seen an explosion of nations and nationalism, a striving by peoples all over the world to achieve national autonomy at almost any price. This transformation collides with all forms of universalism and colonial empire building. Whatever the attraction of communist ideology to revolutionaries while they are plotting wars of national liberation, and however much assistance they may receive from the Soviet Union, the forces of national autonomy eventually come to assert themselves, threatening the client status of the new nation in relation to the Soviets.

The Yugoslavian experience was the first demonstration that the postwar communist world was not monolithic and that nationalist aspirations could be stronger than communist ideology. In Hungary in 1956 and in Czechoslovakia in 1968, Soviet tanks were needed to repress nationalist urges. The Vietnam War, one of the worst political mistakes in U.S. history, was conducted mainly to contain the Chinese, on the premise that the communist threat was monolithic. The United States badly underestimated the strength of North Vietnam's nationalism and how this factor served to alienate the North Vietnamese from China. We also failed to grasp that the long history of North Vietnamese enmity toward China was far stronger than the fraternal relationship of two communist countries. If we understood then as we do now how *unmonolithic* the communist world is, the war in Vietnam might never have been fought.

With President Nixon's historic opening to the People's Republic of China, U.S. policy came to acknowledge that, far from being a single entity, the communist world was riddled with tensions flowing from nationalist pressures. Indeed, the tense relationship between China and the Soviet Union may be a more dangerous threat to world peace than the troubled U.S.-Soviet relationship. In the view of many Soviet specialists, the Soviet Union fears an industrialized, nuclearized China far more than it fears the United States — and perhaps rightly so.

The experience of China, now that it is experimenting with a market-based economy, is an important example of the power of nationalism to overwhelm a country's ties to Soviet-style communism. And this is far from an isolated example. In virtually every country where the Soviets have been thwarted in expanding their influence, the key factor has been strong nationalist aspirations. These aspirations conflict head-on with Soviet power politics. This has happened in China, Italy, France, Egypt, India, Indonesia, Iran, Somalia, and even Syria and Iraq.

The Failure of the Marxist-Leninist Model of a Command Economy

For many years it was assumed throughout the developing world that market-based capitalism was a passageway to socialism. It is difficult to exaggerate the appeal that this premise had for many nations and movements. Though far from dead today, its influence has peaked and is receding. Nations are discovering the energizing effects of free market forces on their economies — a recent development that represents a world victory for the American way. It is one of the great transforming changes of our times.

Even in the socialist world, the Hungarian and Chinese experiments with free-market innovations have conveyed an unmistakable message: the free market works, often dramatically; command economies do not work well. When socialist countries pay no heed to this lesson, the reason is political, not economic. A command economy, dictated from the center of political power, may not make economic sense, but it has proven an effective instrument of political control.

The trend is for the world's nations to reject their Marxist dogma and to understand that the proper mix of modern technology with a market economy holds the key to economic development and to a higher standard of living for their people. The Japanese experience has been particularly heartening for the Third World. Japan's economic success has proved that the model of a market-based, technology-driven economy can be transferred from America's unique cultural and political setting to countries with different traditions. The economic success of other Asian countries is further proof that the American model travels well and can be adapted. If the United States were to help other countries adapt this model to their own situations, we could win many new friends.

The Gorbachev Era

Journalists love to deride the naiveté of those who thrill to every new Gorbachev initiative, and to lecture them on the theme that Mr. Gorbachev is not really introducing Western-style democracy to the Soviet Union and therefore nothing has really changed in U.S.-Soviet relations.

Certainly the Soviet Union has not become a capitalist democracy, even given the wildest interpretation. The changes taking place under Secretary-General Gorbachev's vigorous leadership have as their prime purpose strengthening the existing system. But this emphatically does not mean that nothing has changed. Let us assume that Mr. Gorbachev's purposes are confined to making the Soviet Union more efficient without challenging the one-party system. The Soviet threat to the United States comes not from its form of governance but from its intentions and ideology. If the Soviet leaders finally conclude that the old communist ideology of overthrowing capitalism stands in the way of present Soviet interests, and that those interests are better served by a policy of restraint in expanding Soviet control over other countries, then it is surely in the interest of the United States to encourage that conclusion.

Most Americans maintain that their principal concern about the Soviet Union is not about its form of government; as we have seen, the majority believe there is room in the world for the Soviet system and ours to coexist. The difference between the systems may prevent the two countries from becoming friends or allies, but by itself it does not make them enemies. The heart of the quarrel between the two countries relates to Soviet expansionism — to its efforts to use other countries strategically to oppose U.S. vital interests. Any decrease in this tendency will be greeted by Americans as reducing an important source of enmity.

In 1947 the rationale of the Kennan policy of containment was that over time the Soviet Union would mellow — that is, that it would abandon its goal of dominating others and cease to pose a threat to Western values. Kennan expected this process to take place in ten to fifteen years. Now that more than four decades have passed, it would be obtuse of the United States, having waited so long, to ignore evidence that a significant shift in Soviet intentions may be taking place.

The conventional method of appraising the Soviet Union is to apply the test of "worst case" — to ask, "What is the worst thing that can happen to U.S. national security given the present and potential state of Soviet capabilities?" This mindset has served us badly: it has been responsible for many of the excesses of the cycle of action and reaction that have accelerated the arms race. At the very least, it ought now to be supplemented by a "best possibility" approach, which asks, "What is the *best* possibility of a positive change in Soviet intentions, and how can it be put to the test?" In posing this question, we would do well to maintain the skeptical mistrust the public insists on. But it would be folly to blind ourselves to the possibility of change.

Mr. Gorbachev has explicitly acknowledged that the expansionist ideology of communism works against Soviet national interests and that constructive, normal relations with the United States will enhance Soviet interests. If such an acknowledgment made no sense, we could dismiss it as propaganda. But from an objective standpoint, it may be a valid conclusion. The policy of expanding domination over other countries and thereby engaging the United States in a power struggle with ideological overtones *has* been destructive to Soviet interests. From their point of view, a policy of constructive relations within which peaceful competition can be pursued could prove far sounder. We should not rule out the possibility that the Soviets' analysis of their self-interest is moving in this direction.

The Principle of Common Security

"Security in the nuclear age means common security": this is the conclusion of the Palme Commission report, the work of high-level officials and policy makers from seventeen nations, including the United States and the Soviet Union.[1] The report states unequivocally that "it is of paramount importance to replace the doctrine of mutual deterrence. Our alternative is common security."[2]

Since the report became public in 1982, the principle of common security has caught on at the highest levels of government on both sides of the Iron Curtain, although it has not received much popular attention in the United States. It was endorsed by President Reagan and Secretary-General Gorbachev at their 1985 Geneva summit meeting. Indeed, agreement that common security should govern relations between the two countries was the Geneva summit's major accomplishment. The theme resurfaced in the arms reduction proposals discussed at the 1986 summit at Reykjavik. The Reykjavik proposals startled the world, but they should not have done so: what was shocking about them was simply that they reflected a principle agreed to a year earlier rather than traditional concepts of security.

What does "common security" really mean? At the most basic level, it means that one country will not seek to strengthen its own security by diminishing that of another. On closer examination, this concept proves to be ambiguous, difficult, and opaque, but it is so fundamental that we must struggle with its difficulties. How, for example, can the administration reconcile it with the Reagan Doctrine? The thrust of the Reagan Doctrine is to take the offensive against the Soviets and regain a decisive advantage over them, with an ultimate view to destabilizing communist control of the Soviet Union. From the Soviet perspective, this strategy is based on "zero-sum security": the practice of enhancing one's own security at the expense of one's adversary. For Mr. Reagan to support both the Reagan Doctrine and common security at the Geneva summit and at Reykjavik was either a flat contradiction or, at the very least, an indication that the meaning of common security is exceedingly unclear.

Similar considerations apply to the Soviet position. For decades the Soviets have pursued their quest for absolute security at the expense of everyone else's security. If they are serious about common security, they must abandon most of their recent policies and practices.

If both the United States and the Soviet Union are now prepared to embrace common security, as they claim, then something new and radical has indeed been introduced into the relationship. Ultimately, it will transform both American and Soviet policy. If, however, either side or both are using the concept merely to win points on the propaganda or public relations front, then we have regressed to the dangerous patterns of the Cold War.

At present the truth may lie in between these extremes. The chances are that neither country is ready yet to accept the radical implications of common security. It is too great a departure from the practices of the past. Clearly, however, there is more than propaganda here. In the policy's contradictions we are witnessing neither a gross failure of logic nor a cynical manipulation of world opinion (although some elements of both are present). In the U.S.-Soviet endorsement of common security we find ourselves in the presence of one of those new ideas that take decades to unfold but eventually change the world. The history of ideas is full of instances of the introduction of an idea and long lags in the time it takes to clarify itself, reveal its implications, and give people and institutions a chance to adjust.

A mere decade ago both the United States and the Soviet Union officially endorsed the military doctrine that it was possible to fight a nuclear war and win it. By the 1980s both heads of government had abandoned this doctrine as official policy (even though operating policies and individuals still hang onto it). In both countries the official doctrine now is that there can be no winners in a nuclear war. In this sense, both can be said to recognize the need for some form of common security to prevent a nuclear war. The difficulty is that it is not enough to acknowledge common security as a principle. As a retired Soviet general observed, "If you merely acknowledge the principle of common security, you have not solved anything. What is needed is concrete measures."[3] And that is what is lacking today: in practice, most concrete policies (U.S. and Soviet) either ignore common security or violate it.

Discussions of the nuclear arms race have always been haunted by Einstein's prescient comment after the first explosion of a nuclear bomb that "everything has changed except our thinking." It has taken the world more than forty years to begin to change its thinking and to realize that the old concept of security as a zero-sum game has been rendered obsolete. It will take us until the end of the century to absorb fully the new reality that if we are to survive, common security is inevitable.

Assuming some minimal sincerity on the part of the two leaders at Geneva and Reykjavik, these summits reflected the intent to replace existing policies with specific new policies based on common security. Unfortunately, both countries are loath to acknowledge the extent to which present policies (such as the Reagan and Brezhnev doctrines) violate the principle. The transition period is a dangerous one. It tempts policy makers to take half measures that confound the two concepts of security. A policy that is part zero-sum security and part common security would be destabilizing; it is better to have all one or the other than a mishmash of the two.

What will happen in the future is problematic. Pessimists (calling themselves realists) predict that the two countries will slide backward toward zero-sum security or, worse, toward some awkward mix of the old and the new. But optimists can point to a window of opportunity for moving decisively toward common security. The opportunity, which may last as long as a decade or as little as a year or two, is to think through the implications of a genuine policy of common security and, in negotiations with the Soviets, to begin to align policies and practices with it.

What Common Security Does Not Mean

In clarifying the meaning of common security, we need to understand what it does not mean as well as what it does imply. First and foremost, it does not mean that the United States is obliged to take responsibility for guaranteeing or improving the security of the Soviet Union and the Warsaw Pact nations. The United States is responsible only for its own security and that of its allies. It follows that common security does not oblige the United States to make allies of its adversaries. For years to come we may be destined to remain fierce competitors with the Soviets, but under common security we are obliged to worry about the impact of our actions on their security.

At first glance there appears to be something counterintuitive about the idea — that is, about being required to worry that our actions might jeopardize the security of our opponent. But on closer scrutiny the concept jibes well with common sense; it is sensible to take into account the reaction of the other side to our actions. If we know in advance that our opponent will do whatever it must to counter our next move, and if we realize that this cycle of action and automatic reaction severely reduces our security, then it is sheer stupidity to persevere in such a self-defeating pattern. Why not pause for a moment and learn what it takes to break the cycle, with the sole purpose of enhancing our own security?

There is something else that common security does not mean. It does not necessarily imply the elimination of nuclear weapons. A strong argument has been urged that total nuclear disarmament by the United States and the USSR in today's world might diminish the security of both countries, since it would leave them prey to nuclear blackmail from other nations. Also, we cannot dismiss the powerful argument that we cannot "uninvent" nuclear weapons — the knowledge of how to make them cannot be banished by treaty, and there is virtually no way to prevent cheating where small numbers of nuclear weapons are concerned. Fortunately, it is possible to take these considerations into account while radically reversing the nuclear arms race. Massive reductions in nuclear warheads and delivery vehicles would still leave enough weapons to perform whatever legitimate security functions they need to perform.

A subtler point is that common security cannot be achieved through the type of arms control agreements that have prevailed in the past. These agreements were more concerned with finding a stable balance between the opposing forces than with reversing the arms race. To the credit of the Reagan Administration, it saw that this feature of arms control was unrealistic. The effort to achieve some balance and some limitations in the growth of nuclear forces has done little more than institutionalize the arms race, giving rise to today's grotesque nuclear arsenals.

The arms control community has argued that without the arms agreements that now exist, such as the ABM and limited test ban treaties, our plight would be even more dangerous and unstable than it is, and that these agreements were the best that could be hoped for under the political conditions that prevailed in the past. This is a persuasive argument, which can be accepted at face value. But with changing political conditions, it is time to shift strategies. Arms control agreements that seek balance instead of reductions have lost their credibility. They were conceived in the framework of obsolete deterrence policies.

Finally, common security does not mean that the United States must in any way neglect its military strength. The opposite is true. From the outset, the main impetus behind the nuclear arms race has been the fear that the conventional forces of the Warsaw Pact are stronger than those of the Western allies; hence the reliance on a nuclear edge. This argument too has merit. Fortunately, in recent years new proposals have surfaced from within NATO that make it practical to strengthen that organization's conventional forces at acceptable cost. Doing so would enable NATO to give up its excessive reliance on a nuclear arsenal that cannot be used without risking world destruction.

Common security might well lead to a further buildup of U.S. military strength. If priority is given to curbing the most dangerous of the offensive weapons systems — accurate nuclear delivery vehicles — the result might be a significant strengthening of U.S. non-nuclear military power.

What Common Security Does Mean

If common security does not mean that the United States has to disarm, or eliminate all nuclear weapons, or pursue conventional arms control agreements, or worry about how to enhance the Soviet Union's security, then what does it mean? Though it may take years for its full significance to become obvious, some important implications are well recognized.

Clearly, common security means that we refrain from kicking our adversaries while they are down (especially if we can't be sure they will stay down), that we not treat them like cornered rats by seeking to exploit every momentary weakness. It is the "kick them while they're down" strategy of both countries that has created the present impasse.

More important, common security means that we give up as unrealistic the elusive search for decisive military superiority. In comparison with all other tradeoffs, this will be the most difficult for Americans to support. As President, Mr. Reagan has often referred to the need for a "margin of safety" and appealed to the public to support his quest for regaining the military edge we lost in the 1970s.

Fortunately, some margins of safety are not incompatible with common security, and should not be regarded as such by the Soviets. One is to develop nonprovocative defenses and to strengthen America's competitive edge in domains other than the military one. This is a significant point: that common security has political and psychological dimensions as well as a military one. It is a serious mistake to isolate military strategy from the larger political, ideological, and psychological context in which U.S.-Soviet relations exist.

The most controversial meaning of common security is the requirement that there be a linkage between a military agreement to reverse the nuclear arms race and a broader political agreement with the Soviets. The premise here is that the arms agreements of the future cannot be pursued in a political vacuum.

Admittedly, the arguments against linking military and political agreements are strong. The opponents of this idea point out that even when U.S. and Soviet interests are shared (as in survival), it is difficult to reach agreement. If arms agreements are further burdened with political baggage (where interests inevitably diverge), agreement might never be reached and the nuclear arms race will advance unimpeded. Moreover, arms agreements should not be considered as rewards to the Soviets for good behavior: they are as much in our interest as in the Soviets' and if not, they should not be pursued.

These arguments prevailed for a quarter century, until their weak point could no longer be ignored: for better or worse, politically neutral arms control agreements have come to arouse intense opposition in the United States. Both ends of the political spectrum, conservatives *and* liberals, urge a strong case against them. For conservatives, arms agreements based on parity deprive the United States of the military edge it needs to counter Soviet expansion. For liberals, agreements that stabilize nuclear arsenals without reducing them merely stabilize the arms race at such a high level that in effect they legitimate and institutionalize it. (Conservatives make this point as well.)

These concerns reveal a serious vulnerability in the principle of common security as interpreted in existing arms control agreements. Such treaties address only one of the two threats that trouble Americans: the nuclear arms race. For the American public to endorse common security, the policy must guarantee that military agreements will not be manipulated to create political advantages for the Soviets (for instance, by encouraging their expansion into Third World countries).

Soviet tactics in the Third World are very clever. The Soviets give their support to local communist parties, who exploit local grievances, which in most such countries are never difficult to find. The perceptive journalist Flora Lewis has described this pattern well.[4] Lewis stresses that "communist influence" and "local conditions" do not come in neatly separate packages. The struggle against poverty and injustice, she says, does not usually have its roots in communist influence. But as that struggle unfolds, particularly if it is long and bitter, the toughest fighters — the communists — gradually increase their influence.

Often American policy unintentionally abets their cause, as U.S. support helps the authoritarian right. Consider the sad history of U.S. involvement in Central America. In both Cuba and Nicaragua, the United States in the past supported local repression, greed, and corruption. Lewis writes: "In Cuba, Fidel Castro was embraced . . . by a middle class grown disgusted with the crudity of General Fulgencio Batista's regime and his willingness to cooperate in an obscene exploitation of their country by American gangsters."[5] In Nicaragua our anticommunist ally, Anastasio Somoza, was so corrupt that he stole a great deal of the $200 million of humanitarian aid sent to Nicaragua after an earthquake.

America's obsessive anticommunism plays into the hands of the Soviet Union. The Soviets wage a skillful game with the United States. Their support for wars of national liberation is what is known as a pawn game in chess: even a single pawn remote from the action can assume strategic importance, and the opponent can be maneuvered into a situation where he or she is obliged to defend the pawn at considerable cost. A pawn game is a slow, patient affair — slower than games that involve slashing attacks and brilliant tactics. But in the hands of a master it can be devastatingly effective.

Psyching out the opponent is a key factor in chess, as in poker, and the Russians work at psyching out the Americans with the same seriousness they put into training their athletes for the Olympic games. Some Americans see this pattern as evidence of a Soviet master plan for world domination; others see it as pragmatic opportunism. Certainly Soviet support for wars of national liberation and wiliness in stirring up trouble for the United States in the Third World are consistent with communist ideology. The United States surpasses the Soviet Union in most respects, but the Soviets have chosen a few areas where they can do better than the Americans, and the game of using the containment policy against the United States is one.

Many thoughtful conservatives see the danger of agreeing to arms reductions while leaving in place the Soviet policy of supporting wars of national liberation. Their view is that if the Soviets can neutralize us on the military front, they will be free to pursue their slow but inexorable progress in taking over one country after another until their advances directly threaten U.S. security.

The United States has two alternatives: (1) to go all out to defeat the Soviets in both the arms race and the political competition (the Reagan Doctrine), or (2) to look to the principle of common security for new ground rules that reverse the nuclear threat and set limits on the political competition between the two countries, especially in the Third World. The second alternative reflects the public's fundamental values, fears, and priorities better than the first.

MAS, Not MAD

HOLDING IN MIND both the public's core values and the new realities, we are now ready to sketch the outlines of an alternative to the Reagan Doctrine. We propose a set of goals for the future. The timetable covers the middle range, neither the short nor the long term. The goals of the new policy probably cannot be achieved much before the year 2000, since we will require the full decade of the 1990s to do them justice.

We call our proposal "MAS, not MAD": mutual assured security, not mutual assured destruction. Achieving MAS calls for the American public to accept wholeheartedly the principle of common security. Voters are far from accepting this principle today; there is a long road to travel. But the principle matches the public's values so well that eventual acceptance seems likely.

The policy of mutual assured security is best visualized as a two-sided structure in which the sides support each other. One side is military; its goal is to reverse the nuclear arms race. The second side is political and psychological. It focuses on rules to govern the competition between the United States and the Soviet Union, particularly in Third World countries, and it addresses the mistrust that now poisons the relationship between the two countries.

The Military Side of MAS

The military aspect of MAS is of paramount importance if the threat of nuclear war is to be diminished. It includes several elements:

1. making radical reductions in the number of nuclear warheads and delivery systems;
2. shaping these reductions so as to eliminate the threat of first strike;
3. adding a stronger nonprovocative defensive component to existing offensive ones; and
4. building the conventional strength of NATO forces in a nonprovocative fashion.

REDUCING NUCLEAR WEAPONS BY
95 TO 99 PERCENT

Most Americans, as we have seen, are unaware that NATO preparations call for the first use of nuclear weapons in response to a Soviet attack with conventional forces. Resorting to nuclear counterattack by NATO troop commanders would in all likelihood take place in the very first few hours or days of hostilities. More than four thousand nuclear warheads are now stockpiled for use in such a contingency. Most of these weapons are aimed at military and industrial targets in the Soviet Union and Eastern Europe. The targets include missile sites, radars, industrial plants, bridges, command and control centers, and troop concentrations. In principle the NATO allies are prepared to use nuclear weapons just as they would any other weapon against all of these targets, however ill-suited to the task and destructive the nuclear weapons may be.

For many years former secretary of defense Robert McNamara and others have argued that nuclear weapons are not like other weapons and have no military utility except as a deterrent. Many military commanders share this view but are reticent in public, since speaking out would undermine existing policy before there is a substitute. But it is an open secret that the primary motivation for adhering to the present policy is not military but psychological. Since the Soviets can't be sure what we will do with all those "unusable" nuclear weapons, they will hesitate, it is reasoned, especially if NATO field commanders are under pressure to employ their nukes or face the neutralization of them ("use them or lose them").

McNamara has argued eloquently and tirelessly for a policy of "minimal deterrence" — confining nuclear weapons to the single mission of discouraging the use of such weapons by the other side. Adopting this proposal would mean abandoning all so-called counterforce targeting — that is, the planned use of nuclear weapons against ordinary military targets. It would also mean abandoning "nuclear diplomacy" — threatening to use nukes to achieve political ends. Minimal deterrence would require a very limited arsenal of nuclear weapons, in the hundreds rather than tens of thousands. It is conceivable that we could make reductions of 95 to 99 percent in numbers of both strategic and tactical nuclear weapons while preserving the essential purposes of deterrence.

REDUCING THE THREAT OF FIRST STRIKE

No fear has haunted the imagination of military thinkers more than the threat of a nuclear first strike. The fear is that one side will have the ability to launch a nuclear first strike that will so devastate the nuclear arsenal of the other side that the latter will be unable to retaliate in full force. The nightmare that obsesses proponents of MAD is the fear that the projected "assured destruction" would not be fully "mutual," and thus that instability in the balance of terror would tempt one side to become trigger-happy.

Clearly, if either side has a first-strike capability, the military balance of power shifts. It is not necessary for the capability to be used. Simply having it is enough for one side to undermine the security of the other. It is thoroughly destabilizing: it tempts the other side to run dangerous risks to head off the menace or to counter it before it develops fully. A major concern of Soviet military thinkers is that SDI could give the United States a first-strike capability; presumably, we would then be free to launch a nuclear attack without fearing effective retaliation (on the premise, of course, that our SDI defenses would work).

One of the great advantages of McNamara's concept is that it enables both sides to eliminate the threat of nuclear first strike. The deep cuts envisaged (in the 95-to-99-percent range) can be shaped to remove this menace. The United States would press the Soviets to dismantle a large number of their land-based missiles in exchange for comparable reductions in our MIRVed submarine-based weapons, where we presently hold an advantage. McNamara writes:

> There is no need to rely on the adversary's intentions: his capabilities are visible. Mutual and verifiable reductions in the ratio of each side's accurate warheads to the number of each side's vul-

nerable missile launchers could reduce the first-strike threat to the point at which it would be patently incredible to everyone.[1]

PROVIDING A SHIELD AS WELL AS A SWORD

In the policy of MAS there is a definite place for a limited version of a nuclear defense. With arsenals of nuclear weapons in the hundreds rather than thousands, it becomes technically more feasible to conceive of defenses to protect command and control centers and communications, and also to insure the survivability of small-scale nuclear forces. In this sense, nuclear defense can be seen as an extension of the existing ABM treaty. That treaty can be updated periodically to permit a better balance between offensive and defensive forces on both sides than now exists, with a view to keeping the first-strike nightmare at bay and also to insuring the greatest stability and security.

The concept of defense appeals to the public, because it is less aggressive than offense. It is difficult to see the logic of throwing away the shield in order to guarantee that the sword will kill more surely. There is much to be said for this common-sense point of view. Once the country moves away from the doctrine of MAD, a defensive component self-evidently can play an important role in implementing common security.

FINDING CONVENTIONAL SUBSTITUTES FOR NUKES

The major resistance to destroying the bulk of the American and Soviet nuclear arsenals comes from those who are concerned that the United States and its allies will be left with an inferior strategic position in Western Europe. In this view, it is the fear of risking nuclear war that deters the Soviets from adventurism in Western Europe. If the danger of escalating to nuclear war is eliminated, then the threat of conventional war is increased — especially if the United States and its allies are left with weaker conventional forces than the Soviets have.

If the United States abandons extended deterrence, with its reliance on nuclear escalation, then we face the difficult question of what to do about our conventional forces. Two alternatives deserve attention. One is spelled out in the report of a bipartisan commission organized by the Pentagon in 1987. This report, titled "Discriminate Deterrence," released early in 1988, plays down the threat of direct Soviet aggression in Western Europe and emphasizes instead the struggle in the Third World.[2] The report argues that for this type of threat, reliance on nuclear escalation is not an appropriate strategy; it warns that focusing on the wrong threat prevents defense planners from developing a strategy that *is* appropriate. The commission recommends moving away from dependence on nuclear forces and instead building on America's technological superiority to develop a new generation of non-nuclear weapons, including highly accurate "smart" munitions and non-nuclear strategic and tactical weapons that can be deployed flexibly in Third World military encounters.

For several years the influential chairman of the House Armed Services Committee, Representative Les Aspin, has studied the advantages and drawbacks of non-nuclear strategic weapons and has concluded that a shift in this direction would serve the nation well, both in reducing the threat of nuclear war and in strengthening America's defense posture. It is worth quoting him at length:

> Almost since the advent of the nuclear bomb, strategic warfare has been viewed as synonymous with nuclear warfare. And yet, while the strategic forces of the two superpowers evolved the way they did, there is no inherent rationale as to why this has been so.

Technology has made possible a new class of conventional weapons that can replace nuclear weapons in a host of strategic missions. Capable of hitting targets both in the Soviet Union as well as in Eastern Europe, these weapons offer the promise that one day the U.S. strategic deterrent can be almost exclusively comprised of non-nuclear strategic systems. Carrying conventional warheads, these systems can fulfill most of the missions presently assigned to nuclear weapons. At the same time, these weapons will never be able to destroy whole cities or carry out "assured destruction."

Since the 1970s, great strides have been made in improving the precision of these systems. In Europe, the U.S. is already exploiting new developments in precision guided systems and related advances in high speed computers and micro-electronics for our battlefield and theater nuclear weapons. These trends support the concept that the objectives of our military strategy can be carried out by non-nuclear precision strikes against strategic enemy targets. All that remains is for these technologies to be combined in any number of designs tailored to specific missions. Such weapons can be carried to targets by aircraft or by ballistic or cruise missiles. They can precisely navigate and aim themselves by seeing and interpreting everything from stars and satellites above to the terrain and targets below, and they bring highly focused destructive energy against their targets in the form of explosives and projectiles.

Non-nuclear weapons, with precision delivery and conventional warheads, have a much higher degree of military utility than their nuclear counterparts. With them, our deterrent would be enhanced. Indeed, one could hold the view that neither opponent could afford to yield a relative advantage in their non-nuclear capabilities lest they risk losing escalation control at the very threshold to nuclear weapons. Nuclear weapons could be relinquished as quickly as non-nuclear strategic weapons could cover their missions, and that replacement might proceed as rapidly as technology will permit.[3]

Randall Forsberg, executive director of the Institute for Defense and Disarmament Studies and founder of the freeze movement, has developed a more radical alternative. She argues against strengthening our conventional forces to compensate for deep cuts in nuclear weapons.[4] One of her strongest arguments is economic: once we eliminate nuclear weapons, we confront the reality that conventional forces are a more expensive alternative. It is useful to recall John Foster Dulles's phrase "more bang for the buck," which was used to justify the switch in emphasis to nuclear arms in the 1950s. Roughly 80 percent of our present defense budget is allocated to conventional forces and arms, only 20 percent to nuclear weapons. If we strengthen the non-nuclear side, we must expect increases in defense expenditures — especially under pressure of our allies' fear that in reducing our dependency on nuclear weapons, we are separating America's defense from the defense of Western Europe and Japan. In addition, Forsberg cites the argument of conservative critics that significant reductions in nuclear weapons can have a destabilizing effect and actually increase the threat of nuclear war by increasing the likelihood of conventional war, which might spin out of control.

In the post-Reagan era, these two arguments reinforce one another. If voters grow nervous about rising military costs as well as about the dangers of a change in strategy, the status quo (with its dependence on extended nuclear deterrence) is likely to remain in place, as it has throughout the post-World War II period. Forsberg's plea is to avoid the dangers and high costs of shifting from a nuclear arms race to a conventional arms race by converting to a posture she calls nonprovocative defense. Instead of engaging the Soviets in a buildup of conventional forces, she asks, why not engage them in a build-*down* of standing armed forces and move toward a minimum force of border-guard armies equipped with short-range weaponry. In addition to thinning out NATO troops in Western Europe, such a defensive force could not conceivably be regarded as a threat to the security of other countries.

Such a change would involve withdrawing Soviet troops in Eastern Europe and moving toward political "Finlandization."

The thrust of Forsberg's proposals is the opposite of those of Les Aspin and the Pentagon's blue-ribbon panel. The Pentagon strategy is designed to strengthen our ability to compete with the Soviets militarily anywhere in the world; the Forsberg strategy is designed to reduce — even eliminate — military forms of competition. Clearly, the momentum of existing policies and attitudes runs against Forsberg's proposals. At least in the short term, voter mistrust of the Soviets would destroy the credibility of any American political leader who suggested that America should let down its guard, even if the Soviets also do so. Yet the arguments against converting a nuclear race into a conventional one are so compelling that the goal of reducing military competition cannot be lightly dismissed. The idea of moving gradually toward a nonprovocative defense in tandem with the Soviets is a reasonable expression of common security. Such a policy can assume a thousand forms, some as radical as Forsberg's and others more moderate and gradual (for example, a partial pullback of troops from Eastern and Western Europe, or the adoption of rules for avoiding U.S.-Soviet armed conflict in Third World countries). Whatever form the change may take, it is important that it be conceived with the principle of common security in mind.

The Political and Psychological Side of MAS

In recent years there has been a flood of articles and books from respectable conservative sources urging that America go after the Soviet Union in earnest — militarily, economically, politically, ideologically — and prevail. Since the Soviets are determined to dominate us, the argument goes, we should get them first. From this perspective, Khrushchev's grim threat "We will bury you" continues to characterize Soviet intentions under Gorbachev.

Most Americans reject this posture. The majority's attitude is that there is room in the world for both systems. But the majority does share the belief that the Soviet leaders have never abandoned the goal of world domination for communism. This primal fear, the public has concluded, is to be taken as seriously as the fear of nuclear war, at least until unmistakable evidence of change in Soviet intentions has been demonstrated.

If the public's fear of Soviet expansionism is to be addressed — and public support depends on it — the policy of MAS cannot be confined to military matters. It must have a political thrust as well, one that confronts Soviet expansionism head-on. (The alternative is the Reagan Doctrine.)

Because the political and psychological components of MAS are so interwoven, we consider them as a package. For example, the Soviets pursued détente in the 1970s and at the same time encouraged national liberation movements in Third World countries. In America, this attitude was widely regarded as deception — proof that the Soviets were taking advantage of détente to implement their plan for world conquest. Whereas the Soviets saw no inconsistency between détente and their policy of supporting national liberation movements, Americans saw hypocrisy, deception, contempt for our efforts to establish cooperative ties, and tactical cunning in advancing the cause of communism at the expense of American security. As a policy, détente was simply too ambiguous: it widened the already huge psychological gap between the two cultures on how to interpret the meaning of words, policies, and actions.

In contrast to the conservative version of the Reagan Doctrine, whose objective is to prevail over the Soviet Union, MAS is designed to promote peaceful competition. The objective of MAS is to compete vigorously and aggressively with the Soviet Union within understood limits that safeguard the security of both countries.

COMPETING IN THE THIRD WORLD

For the long term, Americans can feel confident about the competition between the ideologies of communism and democracy. The United States has most of the assets needed to win the ideological struggle: freedom, opportunities for upward mobility, economic vitality, high technology, cultural vitality, political stability, the rule of law, immense resources, a highly educated and motivated citizenry. These are goods the rest of the world craves. If they are deployed with a touch of wisdom, the United States has little to fear from communist ideology.

The short-term picture, however, is not as sanguine, because many of the tools the United States needs for the competition are not in good working order. There is no national consensus on the legitimate and acceptable uses of force; America has no viable policy on how to work constructively with Third World nations; we have not developed a cadre of professionals who understand the cultures of other countries in policy-relevant terms (only a few scholars can do so); U.S. policy makers often fail to grasp how cultural and psychological factors interact with political and economic ones (for example, the United States failed to grasp the significance of Muslim fundamentalism in Iran, and it underestimated North Vietnamese nationalism in Southeast Asia). With a huge budget deficit, the United States is reluctant to undertake costly new commitments to other countries. At the same time, there is little understanding of how existing resources (military and civilian) can be deployed more effectively. Our nation is generous in good times; we know less about how to manage limited resources to achieve strategic goals.

These handicaps create a dilemma that U.S. policy makers have struggled with since the 1970s. The Soviet Union has honed its technique for extending its influence in Third World countries. The Brezhnev doctrine, which Moscow has never repudiated, justifies the use of military force in coming to the aid of the Soviet Union's Marxist-Leninist clients. In effect this means that once a country has become part of the Soviet bloc, it cannot leave.

To draw countries into its bloc, the Soviet Union operates an immense network of relationships with, and training facilities for, vanguard communist parties in the Third World. Once a revolutionary government is established, the East Germans assist in training an internal security apparatus that keeps the communists in power, irrespective of the narrowness of their base of popular support. More than any other factor, the success of the Soviets in expanding in this way and the seeming irreversibility of this pattern have poisoned the relationship between the United States and the USSR.

Since the mid-1970s the Soviets have applied this formula in Angola (1975), Ethiopia (1977 to 1978), Cambodia (1978), Afghanistan (1979), Nicaragua (1982), and other places, such as South Yemen and Mozambique. Usually the military aid is given through intermediaries such as Cuba and North Vietnam, but it is Soviet support that really counts; Mr. Brezhnev boasted of this.[5] Once Marxist-Leninist regimes have been established in weak countries, they become instruments of Soviet military policy. This can be a significant asset: it gives the Soviets new, advantageous military facilities.

The inability to counter this strategy has frustrated American policies for years. (It gave rise to the Reagan Doctrine, and it jeopardized arms negotiations.) U.S. policy makers grow impatient with the complexity of local situations. All too often they prove oversensitive to signs of Soviet influence and underresponsive to everything else. When the United States is able to support a moderate, democratic faction that also happens to be firmly anticommunist, American policy can be effective and free of ambivalence. The crunch comes when the democratic alternative is less vigorous in its anti-communism than some authoritarian faction is.

The reason the United States gets so tense about any possibility of a Marxist-Leninist government is the presumption that the move is irreversible. This is stated well by Aaron Wildavsky:

> Everywhere a full-fledged Communist-Leninist regime has been established, as in Cuba or North Vietnam, it has stayed in power by itself or, as in Poland, with the backing of the Soviet Union. Even a single reversal of Leninist rule would be important, for if it could be shown that regimes can change back again so that the gains are temporary, the importance of particular Soviet victories would be diminished. . . . So far, however, nothing of the sort has occurred.[6]

Think about Cuba. If, whenever a Third World country joined forces with the Soviets in the manner of Fidel Castro's Cuba, the United States had to accept that reality on a permanent basis, the situation would soon grow intolerable. For a small, poor country, Cuba has caused the United States an astonishing amount of trouble. North Vietnam, another small, poor country, has caused even more. So has North Korea. No wonder our policy makers cannot feel complacent about a prospect of more Cubas, more North Vietnams, more North Koreas.

But we should recall that American interventions to thwart these governments were not great successes, despite their cost in money and lives. Castro is alive and well and more entrenched than in earlier years. The North Vietnamese have worked their will on South Vietnam, our ally. The North Koreans are as strong and intransigent as ever. Current U.S. policy, primarily military and stressing military support for counterinsurgency, is to get involved in Third World countries only after a communist threat appears, and then to focus on the threat to U.S. interests rather than on the interests of the country itself. Thus people in these nations are often skeptical about American motives and policies. The United States is believed to favor the status quo, and in many Third World countries the status quo means authoritarian government, deprivation, poverty, and exploitation.

When unpopular governments that have been our anti-communist allies — like those of the shah in Iran, Batista in Cuba, and Somoza in Nicaragua — fall, U.S. policies get buried along with them. When we lose, we lose more than political influence: we lose our moral standing, because we have betrayed American ideals for a "realism" that turns out not to be so realistic after all. If only for pragmatic reasons, apart from American ideals, the United States must be seen to offer Third World countries something positive, and not just the use of their homelands as arenas for fighting Soviet influence.

What do Third World countries want from the United States that we can realistically give them? Many officials in these countries say, in effect, "We want your technology without your culture." There are several ways to interpret this sentiment. Some Third World leaders do reject the individualism and materialism they associate with American life. Others value their own traditions and fear that if they borrow too much from the West, they will undermine their own cultures. Yet whatever other countries do *not* want from the United States, there is little doubt about what they *do* want: America's economic system and technology, adapted to meet their own needs. The failure of Marxist-Leninist command economies and the successes of market-based economies make a powerful argument for U.S. economic strategies.

Nor is the appeal of the United States confined to our technology and economic development. Whatever Third World officials may say, American culture exerts a powerful influence all over the world. American music, television, and films, American social movements, American lifestyles, American products all draw the world's attention to the American scene. The comments of foreign observers are sometimes critical or condescending, but the effervescence, vitality, and creativity of American culture are not lost on the peoples of the world; nor is the link between this vitality and political freedom. It may not always be clear to others how they can benefit from these things, but they exercise an unending fascination.

How *can* Third World countries benefit from America's vitality? To what extent is our culture transferable, and under what conditions? How willing are Americans to help others derive these benefits? What role would helpful policies have in American strategies for regulating its rivalry with the Soviet Union? What weight should we give to these approaches, as compared with military power?

These questions must be answered with enough specificity for us to flesh out a practical policy for the future. However long it takes, the goal should be to restructure American policy so that its positive elements are more than an afterthought grafted onto a negative policy of opposing Soviet influence. Our policies should convey to the Third World the message that good relations with the United States can bring them more benefits than they receive by throwing their lot in with the Soviets. The United States stands for values other peoples respect and want for themselves, and the United States and its allies can help others to achieve these values. America must be responsive to the dreams and aspirations of other peoples. In return, however, it should expect quid pro quos in the form of friendship, influence, good will, support.

Some of America's most successful policies, it should be noted, have involved a minimalist, noninterventionist approach. Formerly neutralist countries such as India, Egypt, Somalia, Indonesia, and Algeria at one time courted Marxism-Leninism and found common ground with the Soviets on foreign policy. But the United States had the forbearance not to be lured into the Soviets' pawn game. Eventually, strong leaders and their internal nationalist development led these countries to become independent of the Soviets and to pursue policies that do not threaten U.S. interests.

Every Third World country requires its own approach. In some instances military force may be justified. (These will not be frequent: there is too much American voter resistance, and besides, it is in the military domain that the Soviets are strongest.) When military force is applied, however, it should be part of a larger strategy that features positive economic and political incentives.

In offering incentives to Third World Marxist governments (for example, food to Ethiopia), the United States must judge whether these will be exploited against our national interests. Each occasion has its own special circumstances (such as the moral imperative to feed starving people). But in all instances the test should be whether U.S. support serves to strengthen the autonomy of the Third World nation as well as to serve U.S. interests.

COMPETING IN EASTERN EUROPE

In a nationalistic world, there is something blindly obsolete about Soviet imperialism. The time has long passed for any one country to control the destiny of others. The frequent failure of the Soviet Union to distinguish between its own interests and the interests of its allies has caused it one headache after another. The worst mistake America can make is to copy Soviet tactics and to attempt to match Soviet puppets with our own puppets by supporting "freedom fighters" whose dedication to freedom is suspect.

The Reagan Doctrine has been a strategy for fighting fire with fire — in effect, by copying Soviet tactics of using force through proxies and subversion. The alternative that MAS offers is to induce both sides to back off. The logic is the same as in relation to the arms race: if either side fails to take into account the reaction of the other, both sides may end up with less security.

Fortunately, the timing for a common security approach on the political and psychological front seems promising. Soviet words are not always a reliable guide to Soviet behavior, but if history is a guide, we should not dismiss lightly the statements of policy changes made at important meetings such as the Twenty-seventh Party Congress in 1985. It was on this occasion that Mr. Gorbachev stated that class interest (the ideological commitment of communism) must be made subordinate to peace (agreements of common security with the United States). Since that meeting, Mr. Gorbachev's policies and actions appear to be consistent with this shift in Soviet doctrine.

In political matters timing is all-important. It is possible that in the pre-Gorbachev years, the United States could not succeed in negotiating "rules of prudence" with the Soviet Union. But now the timing appears more propitious. New rules of prudence would have to reflect a willingness on both sides to refrain (in the words of Senator Albert Gore, Jr.) from "seeking advantage beyond a certain point."[7]

What is that point? Principally, it relates to restraint in the use of force, directly or through proxies and subversion. Neither side should use force or subversion to make it impossible for the other to play a constructive role in any third country

— to carry on normal political, commercial, and cultural relations. The cardinal consideration in shaping new rules of prudence is to respect the autonomy of the third country. If the United States were able to reach such an understanding with the Soviet Union and to correlate it with arms agreements, then the forces of nationalism in the world would do the rest. Nationalism is critical in this scenario, especially in regard to competition in the Eastern European nations that constitute the Warsaw Pact.

Nationalism is an unavoidable reality of the contemporary world. It has good features: it expresses people's aspirations for greater autonomy in shaping their own destiny. It has bad features: it can stimulate a blind chauvinism that threatens world order. But good and bad, nationalism is the most powerful force operating in the world arena; in the long run, it is far more powerful than Soviet or U.S. arms. Only nationalism can curb Soviet expansionism, just as it has curbed other forms of imperialism and colonialism.

Chinese nationalism, Yugoslavian nationalism, Egyptian nationalism, Finnish nationalism, Austrian nationalism — these have already established a pattern that works against Soviet empire building. Nationalism in Poland and Afghanistan has caused the Soviets severe trouble, and will continue to do so. North Vietnamese and Cuban nationalism have worked thus far in the Soviet favor. But this is partly because of American obduracy: we have wanted as little to do with these "difficult" countries as possible, and consequently have missed any opportunities that might have encouraged them to take a more independent path. East German nationalism is beginning to assert itself; how it evolves in relation to the people's yearnings for greater unity with West Germany is a question of great strategic moment.

The goal of common security need not, therefore, mean acceptance of the external Soviet empire and spheres of influence. And here is where the differences between the old containment policy and MAS come into sharpest focus. The Soviet Union has learned how to thwart the containment policy. Containment, balance of power, and spheres of influence are old, familiar concepts of European diplomacy that the Russians understand very well. They know how to manipulate these ideas, particularly how to use military power to win political ends. But the United States is not obliged to acquiesce in the fiction that the Soviet sphere of influence is monolithic and that satellite countries are the property of the Soviet Union. Such an approach would imply that the nationalism of these countries is a negligible factor.

Eight countries in Eastern Europe are formal allies of the Soviet Union, bound to it by treaties and by Soviet military power. Fifteen Third World nations, including Cuba, are Marxist-Leninist allies of the Soviet Union. Many paths are open to the United States for establishing good relations with countries now in the Soviet orbit. Potentially, the range of relations is very broad. Between an aggressive policy of military "rollback" and the other extreme of totally ignoring these countries as off-limits for U.S. policy there lies a world of fruitful possibilities. In the past the United States has explored some of these, first with Yugoslavia when, under Tito, it broke formally with Moscow, and later with Poland, Hungary, and other East European satellites. Rules of prudence dictate that the United States should not lurch into producing crises of security in the Soviets' existing sphere of influence — for example, in Poland or even Cuba. But a long-term strategy should not assume that the division of Europe is a permanent arrangement, or that countries such as Cuba and North Vietnam are permanent instruments of Soviet foreign policy without nationalist aspirations.

In short, we are proposing a strategy of vigorous long-term competition *behind* the Iron Curtain as well as in front of it.

In recent years the Iron Curtain has grown so porous that it lies well within the means of the United States to assist the clients of the Soviet Union, and other nations, in finding new ways to express their nationalist aspirations.

There is disagreement in American policy circles on how best to carry out this competition. Some urge working with the Soviet-favored leaders, such as General Jaruzelski in Poland and Rumania's president, Nicolae Ceausescu. Others argue that conferring legitimacy on Soviet-based authority is precisely the wrong way to foster desired change in Eastern Europe.

The policy of MAS is based on the principle that the long-term interest of the United States is best served by supporting the autonomy of other nations, even when it is not always in our short-term interest to do so. If there is consensus on this point, then the disagreement about whether to work with the official powers or against them becomes a tactical question to be decided on a case-by-case basis, rather than a question of strategy and principle.

Encouraging nationalism is a risky policy. But it is less risky than containment, because military considerations become less important. In reaching out to countries behind the Iron Curtain, America should realize that military factors are secondary. We have in mind a competition in which the United States brings to bear its full panoply of economic, political, and cultural advantages. Instead of competing with the Soviets exclusively in their one area of strength — military force — the United States should focus on the areas of *our* greatest strength — our values and economic and technical capabilities. We should seize the initiative rather than play a defensive game.

Military strength is of course indispensable to U.S. diplomacy. In a lawless world the United States must effectively project its military power. But the present combination of awesome military capability and implacable anticommunist ideology is so frightening to people in other countries that it helps the Soviets by blunting America's moral and economic appeal. The strategy of aligning ourselves with the thrust of world nationalism is not a negative anticommunism but a policy of positive support for people's aspirations for nationhood. In domestic matters our values stress pluralism and individual autonomy. Why should we not support these same values in other nations as well?

THE MISTRUST ISSUE

How realistic is this vision of peaceful competition? The chances, we believe, are surprisingly good — with two qualifications. One relates to time. We need time to give the idea of common security a chance to sink in. It is not yet a familiar idea to the American people. Its ramifications have not been spelled out. It will take a decade or more for this concept to be fully digested as the basis for a new national consensus. Given a decade, we believe this will happen, because the common security principle matches the underlying values of the public.

The other qualification relates to the problem of mistrust. American mistrust of the Soviets is so pervasive that it can wreck the type of agreement envisaged in MAS. However compelling the idea of common security may be, it is unlikely that progress will be made on the political and military fronts unless we can find ways to cope with mistrust. It will not go away by itself, nor will it be dispelled in the near future. We have seen that one of the public's four demands is that the United States should not link its security to policies that depend on trusting the Soviets to keep their end of the bargain.

The "credibility gap" exists on both sides of the Iron Curtain: the Soviets mistrust our intentions and actions almost as much as we mistrust theirs. This is not an easy fact for most Americans to accept, but the public does acknowledge that America must share the blame with the Soviets for the tensions between the two countries. Many experts believe that the history of U.S.-Soviet relations is one of missed opportunities. To the extent that this is so, mistrust has been the spoiler.

Given this situation, the question becomes whether we and the Soviets can develop a policy of common security that does not depend heavily on trust. There are grounds for optimism. Doing business under conditions of mistrust is far from impossible; indeed, it is the dominant mode of conducting affairs in the world. But it requires us to address mistrust with a certain psychological sophistication, which is now absent in U.S.-Soviet relations. The key is to learn how to work around the problem and not let it become insuperable.

Some relationships depend utterly on trust; others thrive even when trust is minimal. The reason lawyers insist on written contracts, backed by law, is all-pervasive mistrust. Business corporations claim that they trust their employees, but they wouldn't dream of doing business without comptrollers and auditors to check everything; there are even outside auditors, whose job is to check on the inside auditors. The reality is that most transactions in the world, especially business transactions, are based not on trust but on what might be called "institutionalized mistrust" — institutions that permit transactions to proceed.

Until recently, Soviet resistance to U.S. pressure for intrusive procedures to verify arms control agreements has prevented these kinds of safeguards from being established. But the new willingness of the Soviets to permit on-site inspection helps to create control mechanisms that do not depend on trust. Also, current scientific monitoring techniques, especially satellite surveillance, make technical verification of gross violations more feasible than in the past (not, to be sure, for all new weapons systems). Other institutions, such as the U.S.-Soviet Standing Consultative Committee, have worked well in dealing with complaints about violations — when the committee has had the opportunity to do its work.

Without minimizing the difficulty of verification, we make the point that if the political will is present, ways can be found around the problem of mistrust. In international relations, unlike corporate business or the practice of law, no satisfactory form of institutionalization exists to cope with mistrust. Here are some of the arenas in which the problem might be tackled.

Rhetoric and Symbols. Words count. Words and symbols and gestures are all-important in our relationship with the Soviets. In the early years of his presidency, Mr. Reagan should perhaps have joined other world leaders in attending the funerals of Mr. Brezhnev, Mr. Andropov, and Mr. Chernenko, as a gesture of respect. Perhaps the United States should have officially expressed greater compassion for the human tragedy at Chernobyl. Gestures of civility count heavily. The Soviets are prideful; gestures are important to them. Careless words ("evil empire," "gangsters in the Kremlin") penetrate their thin skin. Insults inflame the conviction that national honor is at stake, and prudence gives way to the desire for revenge.

U.S. policy makers sometimes underestimate psychological factors, especially the effects on people of being snubbed, condescended to, or made to feel inferior. This was a lesson the British never learned in their long period of imperialism, and lingering resentment has outlived Britain's positive accomplishments. Americans need to know what the cultural taboos and sensitivities of the other side are and to pay them heed.

Open Communications. When tension arises, America's first impulse is to break off communication. After the Soviets walked out of the Geneva negotiations, there was virtually no contact between the two countries for several years. The summit meeting in November 1985 was Mr. Reagan's first direct communication with a top Soviet leader. "One does not dine with the devil" is an ancient sentiment, but under conditions of nuclear parity it makes little sense.

Most Americans know this. Polls show that Americans would prefer annual summit meetings between the two powers to summits only when there is a good chance for agreement. Large majorities think that an important goal of such meetings should be to increase the number of cultural and educational exchanges between the United States and the Soviet Union. Americans also reject the idea of breaking off talks as punishment for Soviet misbehavior. Although the public was outraged at the Soviets for shooting down a Korean jetliner in 1984, overwhelming majorities rejected the idea of cutting off arms negotiations as a response.

In the nuclear age, the greater the tension is, the more important it is that communication at all levels be increased, not diminished. At any moment of the day or night it should be possible to have unofficial (as well as official) access to key people in the Soviet hierarchy, to explore (out of the glare of publicity) paths for backing away from confrontation.[8]

Having easy access to the Soviet leaders is perhaps less important than engaging in an ongoing, open-ended dialogue in which the two sides come to understand each other's point of view. In the winter of 1987, at a meeting in Moscow, Mr. Gorbachev asked Jerome Weisner, science adviser to President Kennedy, why Americans feared the Soviet Union. Mr. Gorbachev was not being ironic. He confessed to bewilderment that the world's strongest and most advanced power would be fearful of the Soviet Union as it struggles to modernize itself and catch up with the West. From the Soviet perspective, American fear often seems artificial, incredible — and the Soviets interpret such fear as an American ruse to foster hatred aimed at destabilizing their country. American stereotypes about the Soviet Union and Soviet stereotypes about the United States perpetuate a fog of misunderstanding that deepens the mutual mistrust.

This does not mean that we would trust the Soviets more if we understood them better. Perhaps we would not. But at least our mistrust would be based on an accurate assessment instead of the present mishmash of prejudices, half-truths, and distortions. No one grasps this better than Harold Saunders, a former State Department official who worked for more than ten years in the Middle East to build a better understanding between Jews ánd Arabs. His experience made him realize that traditional negotations fail to achieve mutual understanding, especially when cultural and historic differences divide the parties. In formal diplomacy the participants are too busy scoring points to listen to each other. Their agendas are too narrow and specific; their time horizons are too constricted.

Saunders has developed a systematic methodology for conducting the kind of dialogue between nations that encourages the participants to understand each other's values, points of view, and concerns in depth.[9] It is a multistage process. The two sides begin by reviewing their interests and the question of how the evolving political and/or military situation affects them. They continue with an exploration of common and divergent interests, and a shaping of alternatives for dealing with both. They redefine foreign relations as a continuous interaction at various governmental and unofficial levels in sharp contrast to today's pattern of limited, sporadic, restricted-agenda, formal diplomatic interaction. The Saunders process, or its equivalent, is a must in dealing with mistrust.

Rules of Prudence. Well-understood, clearly spelled out rules of prudence are an important mechanism in coping with mistrust. Seweryn Bialer has compiled a list of such rules for regulating the competition between the United States and the Soviet Union. Some of these are now observed by both sides, without any explicit agreement. American troops may find themselves fighting Soviet allies such as the North Vietnamese, or the United States may find itself supporting antigovernment troops in Afghanistan, but a tacit agreement exists that the two powers will not pit their armed forces directly against each other. The United States alerted the Soviets to the American raid on Libya in 1986 so that no Soviet-manned ships would risk drawing fire. There is no evidence that the Soviets told the Libyans. Nor, according to Israeli intelligence, is there any evidence of direct Soviet involvement in Arab terrorism.

As the competition between the two countries intensifies, these rules of prudence will need to be codified and extended. The greatest threat to world peace comes from the possibility that third parties allied with one side or the other will draw the two powers into conflicts where accident, miscalculation, or uncontrollable provocations will get out of hand. The rules of prudence must above all take these possibilities into account, especially in the Middle East, and anticipate what can be done to avoid them. A hotline is not enough. Foresight that leads to explicit precautionary measures is required.

Respect for Sovereignty. Soviet support for wars of national liberation and U.S. support for counterinsurgencies against communist rule directly undermine the sovereignty of nations. In violating international law in the name of a higher principle, they weaken world order.

The principle of pluralism supported by MAS implies that although there may be governments in the world of which

the United States thoroughly disapproves, we are not entitled
to destabilize them, any more than the Soviets are entitled to
interfere in the affairs of others. It should be possible to
reach an understanding with the Soviets for both sides to use
greater restraint in relation to legitimate governments they happen
not to like.

Arenas of Cooperation. For the past several decades arms
control negotiations have been the principal arena — sometimes
the sole arena — for U.S.-Soviet cooperation. Even
when they haven't accomplished much of substance, these
talks have proved successful as a political process in which
the two super-powers are able to establish civil and productive
relations. In a world of rife nationalism, abetted by U.S.-
Soviet competition, the requirements of world order dictate
that the two powers extend their cooperation beyond arms
control.

The most important arenas for cooperative ventures are

- strengthening accord on preventing proliferation of
  nuclear weapons;
- strengthening the role of international law and other
  methods for settling disputes without recourse to force;
- reinforcing the methods and processes of insuring compliance
  with existing agreements; and
- reducing the threat of terrorism.

The Soviets are keenly interested in these and other spheres
of cooperation.

In his seminal book *The Rise and Fall of The Great Powers,*
historian Paul Kennedy reminds us that the great powers of
Europe — Spain, the Netherlands, France, and Britain —
declined when they found themselves devoting a large part
of their wealth to military purposes. Kennedy does not exempt
the United States from this fate; he argues that the

overextension of our military commitments may cause us, too, to decline as a world power.[10]

Whether Kennedy's prediction is inexorable may be in doubt. What is not in doubt is the unpleasant truth that the United States is under pressure from both ends of the commitment spectrum: because our country is a great global power, our military commitments grow steadily, yet at the same time, as we shall discuss in Part II, our economic resources are threatened by vigorous competition from Japan and other countries. Ironically, it has been U.S. policy to subsidize this competition by providing for Japan's defenses. Now, however, economic competition from Japan is threatening the affordability of our existing defense policy.

In the first half of this book we have largely ignored the economic dimension of U.S.-Soviet relations, because it has not operated as a constraint. The American attitude has been that our nation's defense is too important to carry a price tag. But this attitude is now changing. Almost universally (88 percent), Americans recognize that "in today's world, a country's economic power is just as important as its military power in determining its international influence." Most Americans (86 percent) also believe that we can "seriously damage our economy by spending too much money to defend other countries." The public is making a direct connection between our defense expenditures and our trade problems. Eighty-four percent say that "while we spend billions to defend Japan and Europe, they are winning the economic competition and taking away American jobs." An impressive 50 percent now realize that "we are slipping dangerously behind in our world economic position."[11] In brief, then, there is a growing realization that America cannot continue to ignore the price tag, and that something must give: either the American standard of living will decline, or our military commitments must be reduced. We should expect a resurgence of isolationist thinking as Americans grapple with the puzzle of how to meet our military commitments to others while our economy remains under siege.

Fortunately, we are not alone in our struggle with over-commitment. The Soviets appear to have this problem in a more severe form. Unlike our own economy, the Soviet economy is inefficient in almost all spheres except the military. More than any other factor, this fact has haunted the Soviet leadership and has inspired Mr. Gorbachev's reformist moves. The inability of the Soviet economy to support the government's ideological pretensions may have led Mr. Gorbachev to conclude that the Cold War between the United States and the Soviet Union is a luxury we both can no longer afford.

We believe that the new economic concerns of the two military superpowers are indeed likely to end the Cold War and to initiate a new era, one that will be dominated by the principle of mutual security on the military side and by a preoccupation in America with economic renewal and revitalization. It is to this subject that we now turn.

II

More for More

Winners and Losers

AT ALMOST THE SAME TIME that the Soviets caught up with the United States in strategic nuclear warheads, another historic crossover occurred. In 1971, for the first time in almost one hundred years, the American economy imported more goods than it exported. As with the nuclear arms race, this marked the end of an unchallenged U.S. lead. The main cause was the competitive challenge of Japan and its East Asian imitators.

Like the loss in nuclear superiority, America's loss of position in world trade was to prove irreversible, at least in the short term. The balance of trade fluctuated in the early seventies, showing a positive balance in 1973 and 1975, but by 1977 the tide had clearly turned against the United States. By 1986 our trade balance with Japan alone was a negative $55 billion, and our worldwide trade deficit that year was $153 billion (see Chart 37 on next page).

The full consequences of this momentous shift have yet to be felt. In both cases (the loss of an edge in the nuclear

Balance of Trade Crossover Point

U.S. Exports and Imports of Merchandise, 1960–1986

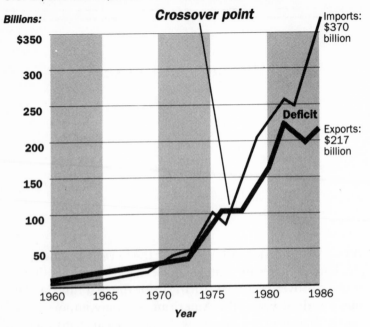

Source: U.S. Bureau of the Census, *Highlights of U.S. Export and Import Trade*, 1960–1986.

sphere and in world trade) the threat is fundamental: at stake in the Soviet threat is American freedom and survival; at stake in the Japanese threat is the American standard of living and political stability. (A sharp decline in our standard of living would create political havoc.) In both instances also the public suffers from its leaders' blind spots. In U.S.-Soviet relations, ideology polarizes the foreign policy community; in economic competitiveness, it polarizes the country's political and economic leaders. The New Right embraces laissez-faire, free-trade, keep-the-government-out, market-based economics. Liberals advocate an "industrial policy" or its equivalent in which an activist government makes the decisions that conservatives would leave to market forces.

The dominance of ideology would matter less if "liberal" or "conservative" solutions matched the country's problems. But most do not. These categories have grown obsolete. The existing liberal–conservative dichotomy has its roots in the domestic politics of the New Deal of the 1930s and the Great Society of the 1960s. It was liberal ideology that constructed the welfare state, and it is conservative ideology that has been busy dismantling it.

The newer realities that concern us in this book do not fit these categories. The problems are too slippery, too complex. Under political pressure, conservative policies yield to *ad hoc* protectionism for industries with political clout and abandon other industries to unfair competition from abroad. A liberal industrial policy, in contrast, would give government an unrealistic role which would quickly become politicized in our political system: members of Congress, bureaucrats, and judges would end up making (for all the wrong reasons) economic decisions that should be made by private firms and industries.

The worst effect of the polarization has been to create a gap between the leaders and the public, which has had a disastrous effect on the public. It has led to confusion and volatility. And it has prevented the public from examining its own values.

Ruben Mettler, head of TRW and a noted business leader, has suggested why our society has fallen behind in worldwide competition: "We simply haven't put high priority on the need and means to be competitive."[1] The difference between winners and losers on the international economic scene, Mettler has observed, lies in the nature of their commitment. Winners are committed to a high national savings rate, investing in the future, developing technology, and pursuing an ethic of quality, responsibility, and hard work; losers are committed to consumption rather than investment and to various forms of government protection. The defining characteristics of winners, in Mettler's terms, are not the skills of economists and financial wizards but the potency of the nation's political will. Mettler concludes: "The global competitive battle is no longer just between industry and industry, or company and company, with each seeking a competitive advantage on its own, but rather a matter of what the entire society does — government, managers, employees, unions, educational institutions, consumers and taxpayers." [2]

It is our thesis that if the nation were truly acting in accordance with the public's core values, Americans would be behaving like winners instead of losers. What obstacle stands in the way, and how can we get rid of it? Finding the answers to these questions is the subject of the second part of our inquiry. The pubic is currently acting against its own values because, as in U.S.-Soviet relations, it has been shut out by the experts: flaws in the experts' framework keep the public from resolving the underlying clash of values. Here we have "consensus interruptus": until people's values are examined and conflicts between them resolved, no national consensus will be consummated.

Unless the American people have the stomach for the competition that lies ahead and are prepared to exert the necessary energy and commitment, there is little the experts can do. Our economic competition with the Japanese is not going to be won or lost by the decisions of a few economists, government leaders, and corporate executives. It will ultimately depend on whether average Americans are truly willing to overcome their reluctance to make the sacrifices and the commitment — as workers, as savers, as taxpayers, and as voters — that are necessary for America to compete better.

If the energy and commitment are not there, experts cannot compensate for their absence by technical agreements on currency rates, trade practices, or tax policy.

In the chapters that follow we show that in principle, Americans are eager to take the winning path — provided that current policies are changed to give them the incentive to do so. To offer that incentive, we propose a policy that can win a national consensus and focus the nation's political will on competitiveness, because it starts with the public's own values. We call it "more for more." It is a strategy for mobilizing the great energy inherent in the American work ethic, increasing the stake people have in their jobs, achieving a better fit between new technology and incentives for jobholders, redefining the role of education and labor, and developing a visible role for government.

The more-for-more strategy is neither the invisible-hand doctrine of many conservatives nor the regulating, directing industrial policy of many liberals. It leads away from macroeconomic policies toward the microeconomic domain of the individual job, firm, and industry. It leads also toward fundamentals: a rededication to product quality, greater efficiency in production and marketing, more entrepreneurship, less financial manipulation, and above all a major change in the unwritten social contract that relates Americans to their jobs.

The United States dominated the postwar era because we had developed a powerful competitive edge in the domestic market and in world trade. There was nothing mysterious or arcane about it: America was simply the world's premier producer of quality products at efficient prices. We gave the best value for the money. What the Japanese did was to find a way to beat us at our own game. They did so in a distinctively Japanese fashion, which we cannot and should not copy. But we should not blink at the fact that they succeeded.

Now we have to confront the reality that there are no short

cuts to regaining the competitive edge. It has to be done the old-fashioned way: we have to earn it through a tremendous outpouring of energy and commitment aimed at restoring America's competitive strength.

In the chapters that follow, we first set the stage by summarizing an oft-told story: how the Japanese became winners and how America has responded — or rather, failed to respond. We then turn to the main themes of our inquiry: what the flaws are in the experts' framework; what the public's values are; how conflicts in the public's values can be resolved; what the main features of the more-for-more policy are, and how it is designed to shape a new national consensus.

How the Japanese Won

IN AN AGE when fashions in economic thinking change with dizzying speed, a theory that is nearly two centuries old continues to enjoy a strange legitimacy. First articulated in 1819 by David Ricardo, the theory of comparative advantage held that nations were endowed with certain advantages of geography and resource and that the international economy worked best when each specialized in what it was best equipped to do.[1] England and Portugal, thought Ricardo, would both gain by trading with each other, even if Portugal could produce both wine and cloth at lower cost than England did. If England had a cost advantage in cloth over wine, it should export cloth and import wine. Portugal should eschew making cloth and concentrate on selling wine to England. Thus each would profit from specialization and from free trade, unencumbered by protectionism.

In fact that is precisely what occurred, and perhaps it is why England prospered and Portugal faltered. Portugal accepted the short-term advantages that specializing in wine produced, and it foreclosed the long-term opportunities in the dynamic new cloth industry. With that choice Portugal opted for decline in economic substance and in its standard of living.

Current history makes this lesson dramatic and meaningful. Japan could easily have been the Portugal of the latter half of the twentieth century. Instead it chose to redefine comparative advantage — for its own benefit. Free of heavy defense expenditures and of the postwar American commitment to open markets, Japan (and the "new Japans": Korea, Hong Kong, Singapore, and Taiwan) concentrated on catching and then surpassing the United States. To do so it pursued a series of brilliantly successful policies and practices in the 1960s and 1970s. They continue today.

Japan has virtually no natural resources — no oil, iron, copper, bauxite, or hydroelectric power. What it has in abundance is disciplined people: a population half the size of America's, crowded onto a land mass the size of California. In a conventional interpretation of comparative advantage, Japan's one natural endowment, its dense population, could best serve as a source of cheap labor. Japanese officials perceived that this route led nowhere except to traditional Asian patterns of stagnation and poverty. They came to recognize that economic theory is not destiny. As Harvard's Bruce Scott has observed, "Japan's remarkable postwar economic growth is based in considerable measure on the Japanese government's rejection of static, conventional economic theories."[2]

What the Japanese did with superb skill was to recognize the changes in the world, adapt to them, and create a new competitive advantage rather than accept Japan's limited resources as a constraint. In Ricardo's time a nation's most accessible resources were limited to those close at hand, usually within its own borders. But in the post–World War II world, there was little reason to be confined to geographic limits.

The Japanese recognized that comparative advantage is not immutable ("you either have it or you don't") but dynamic, and indeed manufacturable.

In the postwar era, thanks to Anglo-American leadership in free trade, tariff barriers were lowered throughout the world. Products moved freely across international borders. Container ships lowered the cost of moving even the heaviest products around the globe. Telecommunications led a revolution in banking, and the movement of capital became internationalized. A powerful international financial system multiplied the availability of money and the speed with which credit could be obtained. (New York City handles $50 trillion in credit a year — twenty-five times the volume of world trade.) Further, new technology was readily available. Although some U.S. companies, such as IBM, guarded their technology closely, others, such as RCA, made their technology available under licensing arrangements. Generally, American companies were casual about the ownership and use of their intellectual property.

The Japanese perceived a unique opportunity. They are intelligent, disciplined, well-educated people. They do not have Americans' unwillingness to learn from other cultures. They understood that although their natural endowment might be limited to people, there was no need to define that resource in terms of cheap labor. They determined to take advantage of the accessibility of resources in other parts of the globe and to use their gifted, highly motivated population to exploit those resources to the maximum.

Consistently, the Japanese approach has been to examine the international product and technology spectrum, to evaluate it as it exists today and to forecast how it will appear some years from now, and then to select a market niche that will yield to economies of scale and to production efficiency. This bold adaptation of comparative advantage has required a strategy that can be applied steadily over a long period of time. The method the Japanese evolved was to upgrade the products they exported to the rest of the world. This took three forms: (1) upgrading quality in manufacturing (for instance, the policy of "zero defects" — making it right the first time); (2) upgrading product value for the money (for example, improving productivity to bring costs and prices down); and (3) upgrading product features (such as the Walkman, the VCR, miniaturizing tape recorders, new features on wristwatches).

There is nothing unique about this strategy. Companies in the United States practice it every day. Many successful companies began years ago with simple products and steadily upgraded their product line. UNISYS, the old Burroughs Adding Machine Company, grew from a firm that produced simple adding machines into an electronic computer giant. More spectacularly, IBM grew from a manufacturer of timekeeping devices and punch cards into today's colossus. The products invented by Edison, Bell, and Kettering have evolved in ways that might have startled their inventors.

What was different about the Japanese approach was the development of a national consensus among the people. To strengthen their competitive edge, Japanese economic leaders focus on one element indispensable to their success: their long-range goal is to replace the United States as the world leader in the commercialization of technology. They mobilize the energies of their people behind this goal.

During the 1960s the Japanese implemented this strategy through far-reaching changes in the culture of the factory. Workers were instructed to participate in quality control activities, which were designed to produce an excellent product rather than the traditional shabby copy. (The Japanese actually named one of their small towns USA to justify using the label "Made in USA.")

Although the notion of participation, like the origins of

quality control, was imported *to* Japan *from* the United States, the Japanese approach is deeply rooted in an elitist culture and is thus management-driven. Japanese workers' commitment arises from centuries of recognizing and responding to the will of their superiors. The genius of the Japanese goal is that it takes advantage of Japanese culture. Japan's novel discovery was to find a uniquely Japanese way to integrate their human resources with new technology within the context of a new world economy.

In its trade practices, Japan can be viewed as predatory and unfair. Indeed, many of our business leaders and journalists echo the complaint of Chrysler's Lee Iacocca:

> We are up against aggressive, potent competitors, backed by their governments — while experts inside and outside our government intone Adam Smith's theories and pretend it is still 1950 in terms of U.S. worldwide economic dominance. Most other governments have realized that the game and its rules have changed . . . they give their industries a better-than-even break.[3]

Mr. Iacocca argues in effect that if only we had a level playing field, we could surely hold our own. Those who agree with this viewpoint can marshal considerable evidence to support it. Through complex and time-consuming administrative procedures, and often through disregard for international trade agreements, Japan (and more recently South Korea) has impeded ready access to its markets by U.S. firms.

But the same evidence that demonstrates deliberate obstruction also reveals a bold, long-term national strategy for creating a comparative advantage that has little to do with obstruction of others. Japan and Korea have progressed because they have combined low inflation, high savings rates, diligent workers, new technology, and high-quality products with a national commitment to strategic industries.

Like Japan before it, Korea has now invested heavily in new factories designed to produce efficient and attractive cars, household appliances, machine tools, semiconductors, and steel at relatively low cost. In a similar way it built new dust-free plants at heavy cost to produce advanced microchips with 256,000-bit capacities, in the face of worldwide conviction that capacity exceeded predictable need and that Korean quality would be relatively poor at a time of declining prices. That perseverance was rewarded in 1986 as the Koreans achieved significant quality improvement. Current judgment in the United States is that Korean chip operations are not profitable, even though quality has improved, but it is clear that the Koreans are here to stay.

Thus the same evidence can produce two polarized views. The first is that the Japanese and Koreans do not permit American companies the opportunity to compete equally — they violate international trade agreements and do not play fair. A very different view, however, is that we are confronting a totally new social and economic framework, although agreed-upon rules are sometimes violated. That framework, receiving sustained support from the Japanese and Korean populations, is different from ours. It seeks market share rather than short-term profits as a primary objective, and, as the means to reach it, determined hard work and patience rather than the manipulation of capital over the long term.

This is no casual strategy. Once committed, the Japanese and the Koreans are ready to see it through, to pay the price. And they do so in an impressive fashion. They learn the language and the customs of the nation whose markets they are determined to penetrate. They fashion products responsive to consumer needs and appetites. They produce goods of such high quality that the old view that Japanese products are inexpensive but shoddy has been erased. In automobiles and cameras, in appliances and electronics and bicycles, in a seemingly endless parade, Japanese products have become inexpensive and wonderful. And the Japanese have worked with unmatched industriousness.

The Japanese Ministry for International Trade (MITI) has been a potent player throughout this development. The principal architect of Japan's industrial policy, it saw the opportunity and planned the strategy. For example, it has prodded the consolidation of the Japanese computer industry, and it has thus been a key target of American criticism for its directive role. But MITI's clout is easily overstated. MITI is the same apparatus that Honda and other Japanese companies have successfully defied.

So far has all of this come that, as a *Wall Street Journal* article observed, "in the typical U.S. town of Davenport, Iowa, people no longer check the labels to determine whether the toaster, sweater, iron, bicycle, or running shoes were made in the United States, Mexico, or Japan. In some lines, you'd have a hard time finding any product made in the United States."[4]

In short, the Japanese did it the hard way. They upgraded their products. They mobilized their people. They merged high technology with high motivation. They saved. They took the long view. They analyzed foreign markets and used government to give their industry a helping hand. And they did all this relentlessly from the mid-sixties to the mid-eighties. When they started on this path, their economy was barely superior to that of the developing nations. A single generation later they have emerged as one of the world's leading industrial nations, a worthy competitor of the United States. Now it is the turn of the United States to awaken from its ethnocentricity and to seek to regain its competitive vigor.

Ways of Floundering

How could America's loss of competitiveness have occurred so abruptly — almost when the country wasn't looking? Were we so absorbed in our domestic affairs and so convinced of our economic invincibility that we could not take seriously any challenge from a foreign source? For twenty years America's response to the Japanese challenge has proven largely ineffective: we have experimented aimlessly, trying this and that, while the Japanese have moved purposefully ahead to displace our competitive advantage in world trade with their own.

Our attempts have taken many forms. The most pervasive has been tinkering with technical solutions. Washington (and many economists) operates on the conviction that a weakening dollar will lower the trade deficit by making Japanese products more expensive in the United States and U.S. products more attractive there. This is a technical approach. But as the dollar declines, foreign investors who have provided the underlying support for the U.S. economy will predictably find more attractive venues. Of the present national debt of more than \$2 trillion, foreign investors hold over \$300 billion. Dollar devaluation has historically triggered inflation and, uncontained, may trigger recession. In the late 1970s, as the dollar drifted downward, double-digit inflation was provoked and a severe recession followed. The danger of repetition is real.

Equally important, this approach, like other technical devices, ignores the implication of long-range Japanese thinking and Japanese willingness to accommodate the currency swing by absorbing part of the loss in order to maintain market share. The Japanese did not reduce their prices substantially while the yen was weak in relation to the dollar. Indeed, they squirreled away large stores of retained earnings and have fed off them as they have absorbed a portion of the currency shift. Now, for the first time in many years, numbers of major Japanese firms report operating losses. Although these losses cannot be absorbed indefinitely, shifts caused by technical changes in exchange rates will not be sufficient to offset Japan's competitive edge in producing quality products efficiently.

Wall Street has also contributed greatly to America's financial woes. Many in the financial community have been preoccupied with making a quick buck through participating in or brokering leveraged buy-outs and mergers. Many have also ridden the stock market roller coaster through historic highs and lows.

Among the analyses in the aftermath of the October 19, 1987, market meltdown, some blamed the budget and trade deficits, and others cited the greed of manipulative Wall Street players. But what the collapse signified above all was that the stock market had been converted from a place characterized by analytical investment to one dominated by massive speculation, hedged by portfolio insurance. The machine had subordinated the person. Technology and the technocrat had replaced human judgment and respect for the fundamentals of the balance sheet, operating results, product performance, and management. Why bother to build for the future through hard work when fortunes could be made through manipulation and tricks? Thus was America diverted; while the high jinks of corporate restructuring absorbed some of our most talented financial people, our competitors concentrated on the fundamentals and built for the future.

Business managers have been absorbed by their preoccupation with getting "lean and mean." Cutting costs, selling off assets, and demanding that labor give back previously won gains are presented as an adaptive response. "This is how to make an industry tough and competitive. This is how to keep management on its toes," it is argued. Yes, that package keeps management on its toes, but principally to defend itself. For reasons we will elaborate later, defending management and getting "lean and mean" have done little that is constructive for our present or our future.

Political candidates looking for an issue have added to the difficulties by their search for a quick fix. Some advocate an exclusively high-tech role for the United States. Others believe that the answer lies in focusing our skills on the two ends of the manufacturing continuum: "We should be the specialists in product design and in product marketing. We can get low-labor-cost nations to load the boards or stuff the boxes." But to yield manufacturing to others is to abandon the essence of what made the United States the greatest industrial power in history. Design and manufacturing are stamen and pistil. They must be integrated from start to finish, or the product will soon lose its character and become like everyone else's. Where in today's look-alike television sets, appliances, office machines, and automobiles is the product differentiation that once distinguished one manufacturer from another?

There is no doubt that if the United States defaults on manufacturing and relegates it to a purchased function from low-labor-cost countries, we can enhance profits on a short-term basis. In the long run, however, this strategy saps the creative energies of a firm or industry and leaves it prey to assaults from those to whom the manufacturing has been consigned. Manufacturing is not like riding a bicycle. Those who have abandoned the skill will discover that they cannot readily get back on and ride away.

Finally, there is the relatively new view that America's future is that of the world's leading provider of services. This argument holds that we are now in a postindustrial era and that we should support evolution to a predominantly private-sector service economy. "Information services carry the promise for our future," its supporters assert. Banking, architectural, computer, and financial services typify the new kinds of work, just as retail trade, manufacturing, and janitorial services typified the old ones. But information services will have few clients in the absence of goods-producing activities. Furthermore, those services may be best employed when they provide input to old industries to help improve their competitiveness. The service argument, if it were to gain the ascendancy, would promise continuing decline in United States manufacturing, wages, and standard of living. It might condemn America to a brief period of hallucinatory success, followed by a long and terribly painful descent.

There is mounting evidence that competition in banking and securities trading is becoming every bit as fierce as that in electronics, machine tools, and automobiles. Japanese banks have already become the leading figures in world commerce. Dai-Ichi Kungyo is the world's largest bank; the next three largest are also Japanese. It should therefore surprise no one that letters of credit cost less when opened by the Sumitomo, Fuji, or Mitsubishi banks than by competing American banks. The notion that we can project a prosperous future in the international trade of financial services is an illusion.

All of these forms of difficulty spring from errors in the conceptual framework of the experts.

The Underlying Cause:
A Flawed Framework

IN ONE of the many Sufi stories about Mullah Nasrudin, a man finds Nasrudin searching for something on the ground. "What have you lost, Mullah?" he asks. "My key," says the Mullah. So the man goes down on his knees too and they both look for it. After a time, the man asks, "Where exactly did you drop it?" "In my house," replies Nasrudin. "Then why are we looking for it here?" asks the man. "There is more light here than inside my house," the Mullah explains.

Nasrudin's answer is an apt description of the reason America has misjudged the competitive challenge so badly: it has been searching for solutions to its dilemma in the wrong places. "Our problems are out there — they deny us a level playing field"; "Our solutions are out there — they know how to do it, let's mimic them"; "Our salvation lies in a quick technological fix, in becoming a service economy, in being faithful to a free-market ideology," and so forth. This tendency to look in the wrong places reveals a fundamentally flawed framework.

A framework works in the same way as a spotlight; it illuminates some aspects of reality, leaving others obscured. At the deepest level, our thinking about the world grows out of assumptions about what is "really real." If we want the essence of someone's framework — where the spotlight is focused — we need to discover what that person regards as most real.

People deal with complexity by reducing it to the few realities with which they are comfortable and familiar. This is a normal human trait; an inability to simplify life would cause us to be overwhelmed and prevent us from understanding anything. But being reductive is sound strategy only when the spotlight is directed to relevant realities. When our framework fails to illuminate a changing environment, an emphasis on the wrong realities leads to mistakes in judgment. When our framework grows outmoded, we resemble the Mullah, looking where the light is best, not where the real solutions lie.

And our national economic framework *has* grown outmoded. Of its various defects, we are concerned primarily with those that befuddle the people and steer them in the wrong direction. There are four such flaws that warrant our attention:

1. a bias in favor of the "hard," technical, macroeconomic factors at the expense of the "soft," human factors;
2. a tendency to add complexity rather than to focus on fundamentals that lead to political action;
3. ideological polarization; and
4. an inappropriate managerial response.

Hard and Soft Factors

Experts divide the causes of disasters such as aircraft accidents into two categories. There are the "hard" factors, which have to do with mechanical failure and other measurable realities. In the case of the Challenger space shuttle disaster in 1986, for example, attention focused on mechanical problems caused by a faulty joint. The other category is the "soft" factors — the human aspects of the problem. In the space shuttle disaster, one soft factor was the "can-do" culture that permeated NASA, which dictated an "A-O.K., we can do it" mentality that sometimes subordinated safety to time schedules. To concentrate on the faulty joint (the hard factor) while ignoring the NASA subculture (the soft factor) would be to impose a distorted framework on the problem.

This distinction illuminates one of the blind spots that has most crippled business leaders in responding to the competitive crisis: a preoccupation with the hard factors. This is clearly illustrated by research findings on the attitudes of policy makers from government, business, and industry. In explaining why America is having trouble competing effectively, the research shows that policy makers concentrate on technical issues such as exchange rates and trade barriers. In fact, these are the only factors mentioned by a majority of corporate executives. Much less importance is assigned to the intangibles, such as poor management planning or a lack of concern with quality.

This view is badly lopsided. To be sure, exchange rates and trade barriers do have an impact on competitiveness. But they are not decisive; it has grown abundantly clear that a weaker dollar and a more aggressive U.S. trade policy will not by themselves reverse the competitive trend now running against the United States.

Economic professionals are frequently puzzled when their models and forecasts fail them. As often as not, these disappointments result from failure to identify and integrate the human aspects of the economy — the soft factors. Consumer and investor values, worker motivation, public confidence, managerial commitment, attitudes toward quality, entrepreneurial inventiveness — the professionals usually ignore the presence or lack of all or any of these, because they find them difficult to quantify and compute. But the "people factor" can never be left out of the equation. The continued failure to recognize and interpret it is a crucial flaw. As Chart 38 shows, the general public does not suffer from this lopsidedness: it exhibits a better balance in taking soft and hard factors into account.

Adding Complexity

Experts can rarely resist adding subtleties to their analysis. They *increase* complexity by multiplying the factors that need to be taken into account; the most serious criticism anyone can make of a technical description is to accuse it of being simplistic. By contrast, in a political analysis whose objective is to mobilize the public behind a course of action, simplicity is a great virtue. Such an analysis must cut through complexity to focus attention on one or two clear objectives, such as "put a man on the moon" or "clean up toxic wastes." A common error is to dilute effort by introducing too much analysis, too many objectives, and too many solutions.

By failing to acknowledge this distinction between a technical analysis and a political one, economic policy makers inadvertently undermine their objective. For example, in pursuit of national consensus, the President's Commission on Industrial Competitiveness inventoried 205 recommenda-

38 Public Emphasis on Hard and Soft Factors

Q. I'm going to mention some of the reasons that are often given to explain why foreign countries are able to sell so many of their products in the U.S. Please tell me if this is an important reason why so many foreign products are sold in the U.S. or not.

■ **Hard factors**   ▨ **Soft factors**

Important:

70%

Subsidies by foreign governments reduce the price of foreign goods sold in the U.S.

64%

The U.S. government lacks a vigorous policy for protecting its trade interests abroad.

65%

The U.S. dollar is overvalued.

65%

American business and government has not made the same commitment to foreign trade that other nations do.

71%

U.S. manufacturing plants have been allowed to become obsolete.

62%

American manufacturers don't put enough emphasis on the quality of their products.

Source: *Los Angeles Times*, 1985.

tions for action.[1] Such a list may be indispensable at the technical level, but, however many items in the inventory, it is fatal at the political level. Many of the commission's recommendations are excellent. Collectively, however, they do not add up to a coherent strategy around which a national consensus might form. There is no single, unifying idea implicit in them that average citizens can grasp and around which they can rally. They are a vast pile of ideas waiting to be integrated into a larger whole.

Liberal–Conservative Polarization

One key to developing a new competitive advantage for America is to define a constructive new role for government. In the 1970s and early 1980s, instead of searching for that role, American leaders were absorbed in an irrelevant debate over which of two outmoded ideologies, traditional liberalism and Reagan conservatism, should guide the nation's economic policies.

Even the most casual observer is aware of the process whereby some economic ideas are stigmatized as "liberal" and "left-wing" and others as "conservative" and "right-wing." A liberal label is usually given to all ideas for greater government involvement in economic planning, proposals advanced by organized labor, and proposals for increased government spending (except for defense). Ideas for strengthening the private sector, increasing corporate profits, and eliminating business regulations are automatically labeled as conservative. Once the label is hung, no further thought is deemed necessary. Partisans know how they feel, and they react accordingly.

There is no clearer example than the debate on the proper role of government in how best to respond to international competition. Policy makers have been locked in a bitter debate between conservative solutions that stress market forces and downplay the importance of government, and liberal solutions that give government a central role by calling for various forms of government-led industrial policy. Many policy makers who argue for a strong interventionist role stress that the United States is competing with countries that give special subsidies to their key industries. Those who oppose an interventionist role argue that if the government attempts to pick winners and losers, it will inevitably distort the workings of the marketplace and worsen the competitive situation rather than improve it. For example, the former chairman of the Council of Economic Advisors, Charles Schultze, speaks for many mainstream economists:

> America is *not* deindustrializing. Japan does *not* owe its industrial success to its industrial policy. Government is *not* able to devise a "winning" industrial policy. Finally, it is not possible in the American political system to pick and choose among individual firms and regions in the . . . way envisaged by advocates of industrial policy.[2]

This controversy has many sources, the most obvious being different interests. The survival of some industries is threatened while that of others is unaffected. Since these interests concern how people make a living — and indeed, whether they will make a living — it is hardly surprising that the debate sometimes grows emotional. The arguments on both sides are almost theological in intensity, and opposing positions appear irreconcilable. Conservatives excoriate liberals, ideologues attack pragmatists, the trade unions question the good faith of business, the supporters of the "smokestack industries" suspect the motives of the high-tech buffs, the proponents of free trade fiercely oppose the advocates of fair trade — and vice versa.

Both sides argue their positions well, but the arguments are substantially beside the point. The pertinent question is not whether the United States should adopt an industrial policy. The fact is that we already have one, and a very large-scale one it is. Astonishingly, the American government has produced more than three hundred separate pieces of legislation or regulation that now give special treatment to one or another industry or commercial activity.

The problem is that the nation has adopted a schizophrenic approach to government intervention. The official rhetoric of Reagan conservatism favors a laissez-faire approach. But time and again commitment to this ideology has distorted the actual policies of the administration and opened a gap between its rhetoric and its actions. As economists John L. Palmer and Isabel V. Sawhill observe, "In trade policy, as in agricultural policy, the administration's free market ideology and its actions diverge sharply, helping the affected industries (steel, autos) at the expense of consumers who are paying higher prices."[3]

In the present situation, the United States lacks the advantages that might come from an organized interventionist policy. At the same time it lacks the benefits that might accompany the working of an unhindered market. Although this debate has been framed in standard liberal–conservative terms of "big government" versus "less government intervention," the world has changed so much that these labels simply get in the way of clear thinking. They force our thoughts away from a vital new role for government.

Any effective role will doubtless cause distress to both conservative and liberal ideologists. Conservatives will be alarmed because government will have to work actively with industry and labor to gain a new competitive edge in the world and also to cushion the brutal effects of economic change on those who lose their jobs through no fault of their own. Liberals will resent the many restrictions that must be placed on an activist government if the cure is not to be worse than the disease. And, given their antibusiness bias, liberals will also resist the many probusiness actions that government will be called upon to take.

A Faulty Managerial Response

A fourth framework defect is the philosophy of management that continues to dominate American industry. One of the key elements of a new competitive advantage must be new styles of management that place greater emphasis on improving product quality and value. Instead of adapting to this reality, however, many managers have responded to today's conditions by manipulating the financial assets of their businesses.

This response is clearly demonstrated by a series of studies sponsored by the accounting and management consulting firm of Coopers & Lybrand that analyze the strategic thinking of American managers.[4] An overwhelming majority of America's chief executive officers (82 percent) see themselves as operating in mature markets. The question that haunts them is "How do we realize profits in industries whose growth lies behind them?" The answer, they believe, lies in cutting costs, in achieving earnings through acquisitions, and in getting a bigger share of a finite market. The code language for this management strategy is the odd phrase "lean and mean," which refers both to specific policies and to a general attitude.

The very words convey the attitude. After the first shock and bewilderment at Japan's success, American business leaders concluded that U.S. industry had grown complacent — "fat and flabby." This familiar defect of middle age was not confined to the body: the mind also had grown soft and undisciplined. Many executives came to suspect that they, or their predecessors, had been seduced by success into lazy habits of mind and had become distracted by their corporations' extracurricular social objectives, lulled by labor unions into taking the easy path of yielding to wage demands even when these were unaccompanied by productivity gains, too indulgent with the growing layers of middle management, and inattentive to the inexorable buildup of costs when discipline is relaxed. To become competitive required trimming away the fat from the middle of the organizational structure and adopting a more hardheaded approach to running business. No more Mr. Nice Guy.

In practice, the lean-and-mean approach stresses four strategies: controlling cost (especially labor costs and the costs of middle-management staff functions); using technology (substituting capital for labor); maximizing short-term profitability (the more robust the short-term profits, the healthier the enterprise and the more secure the management); and adopting a more directive style of managing people and resources (in easy times, it may be permissible to coddle people, but when the going gets tough, tough management is essential). This approach leads managers to adopt a double standard. Their toughness toward an organization that has grown soft and flabby is rarely pointed toward themselves: managers are almost never penalized. Their status and power are usually strengthened. With the lean-and-mean posture, they become more central than before. But those in middle management who are dropped from the payroll are conveniently written off as "dead wood," even though they are often not discernibly less worthy than those who do the cutting.

By implication, this thinking attributes U.S. competitive vulnerability to a minor character flaw. It implies that managers permitted themselves to be lulled by success into relaxing their vigil, but now that the moment of truth has arrived, the inactivity and self-doubt are over. With a sigh of relief, the challenge is grasped; discipline is restored. Morale must be invigorated. The organization must shape up, and all flabbiness must be cut away. In the lean-and-mean scenario, managers see themselves as the heroes in the drama of their firm's competitive performance, and all too often there is no room for other heroes; they need bit players, of course, to provide support, but the power base is concentrated at the top.

Unfortunately, this response discourages most managers of large corporations from taking actions with the long-term future in mind. Making major investments in plant and equipment and in research and development is too burdensome on short-term profits, even if it strengthens long-term growth. Thus American industry sacrifices future growth by letting financial management impose the rules. Typically, the financial approach involves down-sizing rather than building up, buying rather than making, reshuffling players rather than developing new talent.

The most serious problem with the lean-and-mean response is that it ignores the critical role of the work force. Florence Skelly, who wrote the reports for Coopers & Lybrand, comments:

> A lean-and-mean strategy may have an immediate beneficial effect on short-term earnings. But it can also sacrifice long-term growth. CEOs told us that to get bigger shares of mature markets, their organizations must be market driven (rather than product or sales driven). But to implement a market orientation, the workforce — from bottom to top — has to be involved, consulted, convinced, nurtured, trained and motivated to make the shift, or it won't work. The lean-and-mean emphasis, with CEO-as-Supreme-Commander, undercuts this process.[5]

The U.S. economy is undergoing profound changes that are transforming the human side of the American workplace.

Because many managers do not understand these shifts, they are failing to develop our most valuable competitive asset — our human resources. At a time when we need the maximum commitment from jobholders, managerial policies are undercutting people's commitment to their jobs. The phrase "lean and mean" is an apt one: managers are being mean-spirited about people precisely when they most need to be farsighted and large-spirited in their thinking.

The worst feature of this flaw is that it concentrates economic decision making in so few hands. This tendency collides with a powerful combination of forces — demographic, technological, and cultural — that are reshaping the American workplace. These forces converge to place greater control over the factors of production in the hands of jobholders. The ability to improve American productivity, product quality, and service is shifting to the many, not the few. The lean-and-mean management style is out of sync with this new reality.

The People's Values

WHERE DO the people fit? In restoring competitiveness, what role is there for the American public to play? In all the talk about exchange rates, mergers and acquisitions, lean-and-mean management, level playing fields, and trade policy, there is little mention of the public. One of the worst consequences of a faulty framework is that it leads economic policy makers to aim their spotlights almost everywhere except on the American people. That omission, we contend, is a major cause of failure.

A Growing Awareness

Since the early 1980s economic policy makers have been aware of the seriousness of the crisis. By 1985 more than 80 percent of them had decided that America was losing its competitive edge in international trade. In one intensive study of leaders' attitudes, researchers found that "the problem of the

Japanese challenge to American industry arouses more concern among America's leaders than any other social or economic issue in the last twenty years."[1] Thoughtful business leaders and others realize that the problem has broken out of its technical confines and has swelled into a political issue of enormous importance. The Business–Higher Education Forum, a prestigious leadership group, concluded that if the country fails to develop a national consensus on how to tackle competitiveness on a global scale, "it will be increasingly difficult — if not impossible — to maintain a just society, a high standard of living for all Americans, and a strong national defense."[2]

Why is a new political consensus so urgent? The answer is implicit in Ruben Mettler's observation, cited earlier, about winners and losers in the global economy. Mettler sees as losers those nations committed to consumption over investment and to seeking government protection against the storm winds of international trade. That position is, unfortunately, an apt description of American public opinion today. Over the years the American people have steadily drifted toward lower levels of saving, preferring consumption, and poll after poll shows majorities leaning toward protectionism. If public opinion persists in this pattern as the crisis grows more severe, it will bode ill for the country. We believe that Mettler is correct: to fail to come to grips with the root causes of the competitiveness crisis and to rely instead on shortsighted approaches — spending and government protection against competition — is a formula for economic disaster.

If the public were firmly committed to this loser position, that would indeed be cause for anxiety. But the opinion polls do not reflect the people's firm and settled convictions — that is, true public judgment. Today's opinions are inconsistent with the public's own basic values, and in the long run those values will ultimately shape public judgment.

Though lagging behind expert awareness, the public's recognition of the seriousness of the competitiveness crisis has been steadily rising (see Chart 39). Several factors are raising public consciousness, especially the realization that U.S. trade with Japan is greatly imbalanced. Survey research shows that as people grasp the magnitude of the trade deficit, they understand the seriousness of the problem (see Chart 40). In the next several years public awareness can be expected to match the level of concern among experts, thereby meeting an important condition for consensus building.

Polls show that the public's opinions are rigidly compartmentalized — a common feature of mass opinion before people come to grips with an issue. Although competition from foreign products is seen as a major cause of unemployment, the polls show that people do not spontaneously connect the trade deficit with unemployment. For example, in a series of questions, people were asked to rank the five most serious threats to the economy. Almost invariably they ranked unemployment first and the trade deficit last![3] People don't yet equate the two threats, but this is precisely the

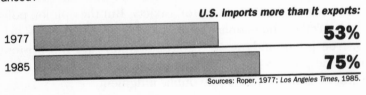

39 **Awareness of the U.S. Trade Deficit**

Q. When it comes to exporting U.S. goods to other countries and importing goods from other countries, is it your impression that at the present time we export more goods than we import, or import more than we export, or that imports and exports are about equally balanced?

U.S. imports more than it exports:

1977	**53%**
1985	**75%**

Sources: Roper, 1977; *Los Angeles Times*, 1985.

40 **The Seriousness of the Trade Deficit**

Q. Now let me ask you about trade bills that are being considered in Congress. The present trade deficit of the U.S. is $150 billion, meaning we are importing $150 billion more than we are selling abroad. Do you feel that this trade deficit is very serious, somewhat serious, not very serious, or not serious at all?

**6%
Not serious

3%
Not sure

*91%
Serious

Q. Last year Japan sold over $36 billion more in products to the U.S. than the U.S. sold to Japan. This year, the Japanese surplus of trade with the U.S. is likely to reach $50 billion. How serious do you feel it is that Japan is selling so much more to the U.S. than the U.S. is selling to Japan—very serious, somewhat serious, not very serious, or not serious at all?

3%
Not sure

**11%
Not serious

*89%
Serious

*Represents both very serious and somewhat serious.
**Represents both not very serious and not at all serious.
Sources: Harris, November 1985; Harris, for *Business Week*, March 1985.

kind of link that politicians do make. We can anticipate that before the 1990s, the connection will be vigorously hammered home.

As public consciousness about the gravity of the problem grows, the question of whether the nation continues to flounder or pursues a single-minded strategy with the public's support will depend on how quickly its policies adapt to public values. Perhaps no single insight is more important for consensus building than a better understanding of what public values need to be addressed by a new competitive strategy. A closer look at public opinion on protectionism reveals how huge a gap exists between people's current opinions and their core values.

Protectionism

Since the 1970s, approximately two thirds of the electorate has supported government restrictions on importing foreign goods (see Chart 41). This pattern has not been lost on some politicians, who see an opportunity to advance their careers by embracing the protectionist cause. But their tactic is short-sighted. A close analysis of opinion polls shows persuasively that the public's endorsement of protectionism could hardly be more unstable. As soon as arguments *against* protectionism are put forward (for example, higher prices, less choice of quality), support plunges from majority to minority levels.

41 Support for the Idea of Protectionism

Q. Should government restrict imports of goods from other countries that are priced lower than American-made goods of the same kind?

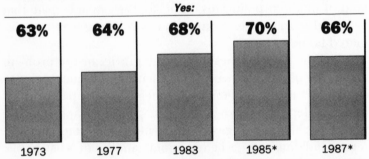

Yes:

| 63% | 64% | 68% | 70% | 66% |

| 1973 | 1977 | 1983 | 1985* | 1987* |

*Question wording: "Would it be a good idea to put tighter limits on imports of foreign products, or would it be a bad idea?"
Sources: Roper, 1973–1983; CBS News/*New York Times*, 1985 and 1987.

One of the reasons that public support for protectionism fluctuates is that the solution doesn't fit well with people's intuitive understanding of the causes of the competitiveness problem. Americans are deeply concerned about what they see as America's inability to keep pace with imports in price and quality. Seven out of ten Americans (70 percent) believe the solution to competitiveness lies "in improving the quality of U.S. products and services with more efficiency" rather than in depending on "trade laws that would make it much more difficult for competing foreign products to come into the U.S."[4] As Chart 42 shows, overwhelming majorities prefer nonprotectionist strategies focusing on tightening our quality standards (93 percent) and increasing our investment

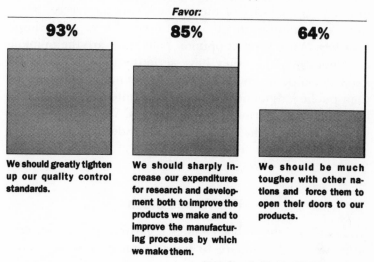

42 Support for Nonprotectionist Strategies

Q. There have been a number of steps or actions suggested to make the U.S. more competitive in the world market. For each one I ask you about, would you tell me if you favor it or oppose it?

Favor:

93%   **85%**   **64%**

We should greatly tighten up our quality control standards.

We should sharply increase our expenditures for research and development both to improve the products we make and to improve the manufacturing processes by which we make them.

We should be much tougher with other nations and force them to open their doors to our products.

Source: Roper, for *U.S. News & World Report,* 1987.

in research and development to improve American products and manufacturing processes (85 percent). Significantly, whenever alternatives to protectionism are presented, consumers choose them. For example,

- by almost a four-to-one margin (73 percent to 20 percent), people prefer "tougher trade negotiations to get U.S. products into foreign countries" to a tariff on imported products,[5] and
- large majorities of consumers believe that the future lies with "computer and high-tech products" rather than in restricting imports from abroad.[6]

The lack of conviction about protectionism is clearly indicated in a survey finding that fewer than one out of five Americans (18 percent) believes that the trade deficit would go away even if *all* trade barriers between Japan and the United States were removed.[7]

The unstable support for protectionism is strikingly similar to that for the nuclear freeze. Recall that opinion polls show that a large majority of the public favors the freeze, but as soon as counterarguments are raised, the support simply vanishes. What present opinion polls show are the opinions of Americans *before* they have seriously thought about the issue of competitiveness. They represent mass opinion rather than public judgment. Protectionism conforms to some public values, but it seriously violates others. Voters have not yet worked through the clash of values underlying protectionism.

The Values Clash

In describing the public's values regarding U.S.-Soviet relations, we used a square to trace boundaries within which policy would have to fit. And we demonstrated that serious failure to meet any one of the four values forming the square would lead to changeable, unstable public reaction.

A similar square can be adduced for public values regarding the competitiveness issue. The boundaries of the square are again formed by four values:

1. protecting American job opportunities;
2. meeting consumer demands for quality products at competitive prices;
3. stringently applying the principle of fairness; and
4. mobilizing the will to win: a fierce desire to see America succeed competitively. (See Chart 43.)

As with the nuclear arms issue, these four values are not easily reconciled with one another. It is no great trick to conceive a policy that matches one or two of them, but it is very difficult to shape a policy that does not run afoul of any of the four. Yet nothing less will insure a solid and stable public consensus.

The most serious difficulty is that these four values harbor a conflict between *market* values on the one hand and *communal* and *individual* values on the other. Market values are those associated with the workings of market forces in a free enterprise system. The use of competition to bring consumers the products and services that give the best value for the money is a market value. Communal and individual values are those that people regard as so important that they wish to preserve them even when they run counter to market forces. On the communal side, Americans do not want market forces to prevail irrespective of consequences when it comes to such matters as health care for the elderly and the indigent, education for young people who are willing to work hard and sacrifice, and help for the small farmer, the crippled, the blind, the mentally ill, and all Americans who cannot help themselves. On the side of

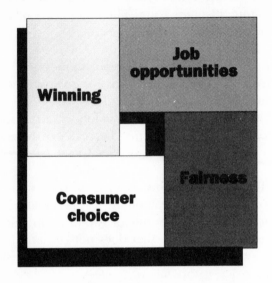

individual values, Americans do not want to be ripped off by business, either as consumers or as employees; they do not want their jobs to be victimized by market forces; and they want to win the economic struggle at the personal as well as the national level.

It is essential for policy makers to understand that safeguarding job opportunities for Americans is a communal value as much as it is a market value. It is, in the secular sense, a "sacred good" that is not to be sacrificed to a mindless social Darwinism created by impersonal market forces. Fairness, so important in the overall American value system, is particularly relevant here. Americans feel passionately that it is not fair for people to lose their jobs through no fault of their own. It is not fair for the Japanese to have access to our markets when we don't have equal access to theirs. It is not fair to close plants without warning. It is not fair to reward executives in bad times while demanding that workers give back benefits. If the present mania for mergers and acquisitions continues, communal values will refuse to yield further to market values, and there will be a fierce backlash against those business executives who apply market values to everything except their own rewards.

The fourth value—the will to win the competitiveness struggle—is both a market and a communal value. Average Americans support successful competition for the same reason that business people do: they see it as the best way to achieve important market goals. But the desire to win is more than an application of a bloodless economic principle; it is a war cry, a whoop of energy, an expression of pride and patriotism, and above all an expression of self. Americans want the country to win because as individuals they are determined to play the game to win: partly, of course, for the prizes, but in no small measure for the sheer zest of the game. To win competitively is to prove to oneself that one is a winner in the game of life.

The tension between communal and market values creates a wide range of cross-pressures on the competitiveness issue. The most severe is between the consumer's desire to get good-quality products and services at the best possible price and the public's communal concerns with jobs, fairness, and patriotism. When American consumers are asked what is most important to them in buying a product or service, quality comes first (78 percent), followed by price (58 percent), followed by "Made in the U.S.A." (37 percent).[8] When people are asked their reasons for purchasing products made in Japan, price and quality lead the list.[9] In comparing American-made automobiles with foreign-made cars, people have increasingly perceived price and/or quality advantages in for-

44 The Advantages of Foreign-Made Cars

Q. We would like to get your general impression of foreign cars vs. American cars of more or less comparable size. I'll read off some qualities or characteristics of cars, and for each tell me how you think foreign cars compare to American cars.

Foreign cars' gas economy is better:

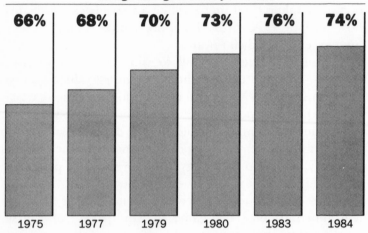

| 66% | 68% | 70% | 73% | 76% | 74% |
| 1975 | 1977 | 1979 | 1980 | 1983 | 1984 |

Foreign cars' quality of workmanship is better:

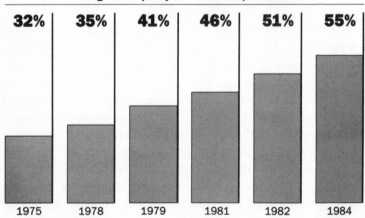

| 32% | 35% | 41% | 46% | 51% | 55% |
| 1975 | 1978 | 1979 | 1981 | 1982 | 1984 |

Figures represent both "a lot better" and "a little better."
Source: Roper, 1975–1984.

eign-made cars since the mid-1970s, particularly "quality of workmanship" (see Chart 44).

All things being equal, Americans unhesitatingly prefer to buy the homemade product (94 percent). But all things are not equal. There are numerous signs that American products are losing ground in reputation for quality and price. One *Time* poll showed that only 25 percent strongly agree that U.S. products are better than imports.[10] For example, two thirds of Americans (67 percent) now assume that American-made clothing comparable in style and quality to imported clothing is bound to be more expensive.[11] If foreign cars are seen to have better or comparable quality at a lower price, Americans are inexorably drawn to the imports.

This pattern holds not only for cars and clothing but for products in general. Preference for buying the American products plunges from 94 percent if prices are equal to a mere 36 percent if the American product costs about a third more (see Chart 45). We see here an example of a market value (product quality at a good price) pitted against a communal value ("buy American"). For most Americans, the market value wins. People see this preference as a test not of patriotism but of common sense.

Market and communal values collide most directly in relation to jobs. Americans are willing to make some sacrifices to save jobs for Americans (see Chart 46), and their protectionist tendencies reflect that willingness. But what the survey data show in great detail is that this willingness to sacrifice is limited. When consumers are asked to sacrifice variety of choice in order to limit imports, opposition to protectionism increases from 38 percent to 55 percent. When they are asked to pay more for domestic products, opposition rises to 60 percent. And when they are asked to sacrifice product quality, people's opposition rises dramatically, to 76 percent! (See Chart 47.)

45 Resistance to Paying More for American Products

Q. Generally, if you were shopping and found two products of equal quality, an imported brand and an American, which one would you choose (given these price conditions)?

■ **Would buy the U.S. product** □ **Would buy the imported product**

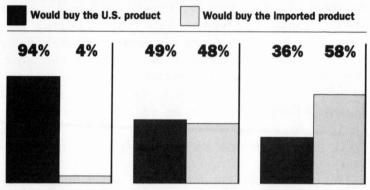

| 94% | 4% | 49% | 48% | 36% | 58% |

Products of equal quality; both cost $200

Products of equal quality; the U.S. product costs $225, the imported product costs $200

Products of equal quality; the U.S. product costs $260, the imported product costs $200

Source: Gallup, for *Newsweek*, 1983.

46 Paying to Protect American Jobs

Q. Would you be willing to pay more for certain consumer goods—such as clothing—if paying more helped keep jobs in this country?*

5%
Not sure

19%
Not willing to pay more to save jobs

76%
Willing to pay more to save jobs

*Sample drawn from registered voters who had heard about the trade imbalance.
Source: Yankelovich, Skelly and White, for *Time*, 1985.

Opposition to Import Restrictions in Certain Circumstances

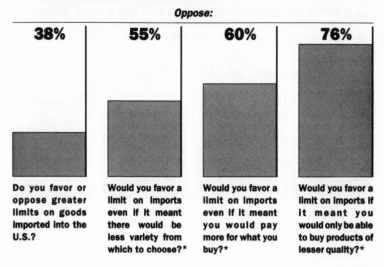

Oppose:

38%	55%	60%	76%
Do you favor or oppose greater limits on goods imported into the U.S.?	Would you favor a limit on imports even if it meant there would be less variety from which to choose?*	Would you favor a limit on imports even if it meant you would pay more for what you buy?*	Would you favor a limit on imports if it meant you would only be able to buy products of lesser quality?*

*Asked of those who favored greater limits on imported goods.
Source: NBC News/*Wall Street Journal*, October 1985.

Since 1973 the Roper Organization has been asking cross sections of the public what they regard as good arguments for and against protectionism. Among the "pro" arguments, the one that wins the most support holds that "restricting imports would mean more jobs for Americans" (see Chart 48). When, however, the public is asked about arguments *against* protectionism, three prove to be persuasive to the majority: (1) "trade barriers create world tension," (2) without import restrictions, "Americans can buy goods at lower prices," and (3) "foreign competition forces American manufacturers to find better ways to make things and to bring their prices into line." It is the third of these that most Amer-

48 Arguments in Favor of Import Restrictions

■ Restricting imports would mean more jobs for Americans.

■ Restricting imports would improve our trade balance—the difference between money going out of and into the country.

■ Keeping out foreign goods would mean American companies would make better profits.

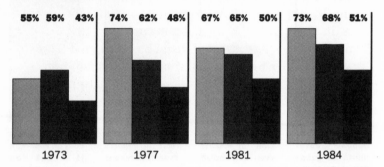

55% 59% 43%   74% 62% 48%   67% 65% 50%   73% 68% 51%

1973   1977   1981   1984

Source: Roper, 1973–1984.

49 Arguments Against Import Restrictions

■ Foreign competition forces American manufacturers to find better ways to make things and bring their prices in line.

■ Trade barriers create world tensions.

■ Americans can buy goods at lower prices.

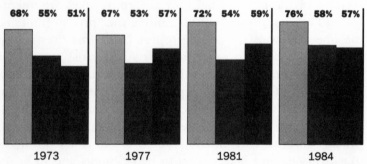

68% 55% 51%   67% 53% 57%   72% 54% 59%   76% 58% 57%

1973   1977   1981   1984

Source: Roper, 1973–1984.

icans support. Moreover, this argument grows more compelling with the passage of time (see Chart 49).

In summary, when the public does arrive at a considered judgment, support for protectionism plunges, particularly if other means are found to protect jobs or if the protectionists' claim to safeguard jobs proves hollow. (The trauma of job loss in the Great Depression, brought on in part by the Smoot-Hawley Tariff Act of 1930, has not faded from memory.) Creating a new national consensus depends critically on presenting the public with policy options that square with all four relevant values better than protectionism does.

More for More in Principle

A NEW NATIONAL CONSENSUS, yes; but a consensus on what? If the public is to be asked to embrace a concept more in keeping with its own goals and values than protectionism, what should that concept be? It must be simple to grasp. It must be credible. And it must balance market values with communal and individual ones.

To meet these conditions, we propose the concept of "more for more." *More*, in this context, has several meanings. First and foremost, it means that many more people need to be involved in the front lines of the economic competition. All of the technical solutions that policy makers have conjured up in recent years suffer from the same mistaken assumption. They all assume that the key players are the few: the experts, government officials, bankers, economists, business executives, and other elites. They assume that the competition is a generals' war, not a people's war. If revitalization were merely a matter of exchange rates or trade policy or financial restructuring, then their assumption would be correct. From a strategic point of view, if a technical solution can restore U.S. competitiveness, it makes sense to ignore the millions of average jobholders who design, make, sell, and service the products America produces, on the grounds that their contribution is secondary.

The many experts who hold this view are not necessarily belittling the American work force. They simply assume that strategically, this is not the major arena for the economic battle. In their vision of what it takes to achieve economic dominance, people don't really matter. What matters is the management of money, technology, and government policy.

The more-for-more concept takes strong issue with this outlook. It claims that the struggle to regain a competitive advantage is more everybody's war than might appear at first glance. It claims that the struggle will be won not in the stratosphere of grand strategy, but inch by inch, product by product, market by market. As stated at the outset, our thesis is that the solution lies in the energy and commitment of the millions rather than in the cleverness of the few.

More therefore refers not only to broadening the base of players but also to the effort that millions of jobholders must give to their work. The economy needs an infusion of human energy and commitment. If U.S. competitiveness is to improve, jobholders must be asked to give more attention and much more care to quality, costs, and service. Consumers must be asked to save more and spend less. Voters must be asked to support new roles for government, such as assisting industries that export American products and services to other countries, aiding Third World economies so that they become better trading partners, and supporting efforts to upgrade the American educational system.

The second *more* in "more for more" means getting more

in return for this effort. The incentive for giving more is the opportunity to get something back. If jobholders give entrepreneurial energies, why should they not participate in the benefits of successful entrepreneurship — as partners, owners, profit sharers? If they give more dedication and devotion to their jobs, why should they not enlarge the scope of their decision making, enjoy bigger responsibilities and greater satisfaction, and have an incentive to increase their financial rewards? If they save more, consume less, and dedicate themselves to winning the battle, the rewards should be both material and psychological: with success, the American standard of living will rise, and the morale of our society will be raised.

The more-for-more concept assumes that to compete effectively, the nation now needs a sustained burst of economic vitality of the kind Americans have experienced in the past. We should keep in mind that sustained outbursts of economic vitality are rare among nations and rare in human history. If we look at our own history, America found the energy it needed in the early part of the century in the millions of immigrants and rural workers who were willing to accept the discipline of the assembly line in exchange for a chance at a better life. In the postwar decades the energy came from the pent-up demand accumulated during the Depression and World War II, as the promise of moving into comfortable middle-class status gave a majority of Americans a powerful incentive to devote their energies to economic growth. Unless there are tens of millions of jobholders who are now willing to exert a comparable effort, the experts and government leaders will be stymied. Alone, they cannot engineer a new wave of economic vitality.

The Economic Credibility of "More for More"

The political strength of the more-for-more strategy is that it exemplifies the four values important to Americans: jobs, fairness, value for money, and a chance to win. It gives a central role to jobs, upgrading both the content of and the rewards for work. In assigning a positive role to government, it seeks to insure fairness and compliance with communal values as well as marketing values. It also focuses on improving the quality and economic value of American-made products and services, thereby maximizing value for the consumer. And above all, it is designed to involve mainstream America directly in winning the economic competition, so that average Americans can take renewed pride and satisfaction in the fruits of their work. Because the more-for-more concept can fulfill these values, it forms a solid basis for consensus building, especially when individual Americans see that there is something in it for them if they respond energetically.

However, a major obstacle besets the concept. Inevitably, policy makers — business leaders, economists, government officials — will express great skepticism about whether such a strategy will work in practice. "More for more" demands a new managerial attitude toward people — a greater willingness than many employers now have to permit employees to share in the fruits of successes that they have helped to create. In many ways this attitude goes against the spirit of the times. Today's version of the rugged individualism of the American past is to grab as much as one can for oneself — that is, to maximize one's own gain. At first glance, sharing the gain with others is, if not an alien idea, a concept that lacks broad appeal.

There is a certain asymmetry in today's social attitudes. When thinking of themselves, people believe fiercely that they are entitled to share in benefits they help to produce. When thinking about others, however, people are slow to acknowledge that others may deserve a larger piece of the pie, especially if it seems to be at their own expense. This attitude gives the present era its aura of selfishness and self-seeking. Indeed, we would be blind not to see the broad streak of self-centeredness that characterizes American life today.

Whatever our ultimate moral judgment, we should recognize that this outlook is compatible with capitalist enterprise. In fact it is more than compatible: it is an outlook that capitalism actively encourages. Since the United States is engaged in a competition that is capitalistic in nature, this attitude is a potential strength, not a weakness. But it requires employers to come to understand that they have a strong business rationale for giving more.

The perfect example is the stock market. This is a place where selfish people eagerly share ownership of their companies with others by selling stock to them. Generosity of spirit, charity, communal concerns — these are not words we would apply to the daily transactions of the stock exchange, whether it is going up or coming down. The stock exchange exists because business has found it can maximize its gains by sharing ownership: the capital it acquires through selling stock enables business to expand and increase profits, and also to create greater wealth for existing owners, *even though they have given up part of their ownership*. This form of sharing lies at the very heart of capitalism.

For employers to share more with employees, they would have to be convinced that such sharing would result in greater wealth for themselves and for their enterprises as well as for their employees. At present no such conviction exists. The major drawback of the more-for-more concept therefore is that it appears to lack an economic rationale. It is not easy to understand why it is so important for Americans to give more to their jobs and why this effort will make such a critical difference to our competitive standing.

When the United States began to lose battles in Vietnam, the commanding general, William Westmoreland, being a conscientious man, kept adding to his workday. He soon found himself working day and night, to the point of exhaustion. Perhaps he believed that by giving every ounce of human energy he could muster, he could turn the tide of battle. He did not, simply because the length of his workday was irrelevant to the outcome of the war. However laudatory his motives, his effort proved futile. With respect to our economic war with Japan, most experts argue that it would be nice if Americans worked harder and to better effect. It might even make a difference, but it cannot turn the tide of battle — especially if American industry has to pay even more for the extra effort, thereby further pricing itself out of the market.

This argument cannot be disregarded. America *is* a high-cost producer. Just working harder, in the sense of putting in longer days and trying harder, could by itself prove frustrating and futile. Working hard in a bankrupt cause will not save it. And even if "more for more" is implemented in the context of a sound overall strategy, it will inevitably encounter the skepticism of conventional economic thinkers, because they do not buy the idea that the key to success lies in the energy and commitment of the public.

Twenty or thirty years ago they would have been correct. But they are less correct today, because they are overlooking an enormous change in the workplace and failing to take its implications into account. American management is accustomed to an organizational hierarchy in which the manager is the key player: he or she takes the responsibility when things go wrong and the lion's share of the rewards when they go right (sometimes even when they go wrong). In today's economy the manager is of course still a central figure. But to an extraordinary degree, control over quality and costs has shifted in recent years to the individual who is closest to the job.

Our most compelling argument is that the American workplace has changed from a *low-discretion* to a *high-discretion* environment, in which the individual's control over his or her own effort and over product quality and costs has vastly increased. In the past, when the Detroit assembly line personified the workplace, the individual worker had much less control over the product. In those days authority was vested primarily in engineers, supervisors, and managers, who planned and managed the flow of work. Now, however, because of a combination of demographic, technological, and cultural changes, every worker, whether a technician, office worker, assembly-line worker, or tester, has more and more effective control over how and how well the product is produced.

This is not an abstract point. Everyone who works in today's economy knows what it means. Sloppy service in the restaurant, carelessness at the local bank or building site, inattention to detail at the hospital or day-care center, poor morale in government offices, indifference on the assembly line: these are the raw materials that produce products and services of mediocre quality. Most Americans take pride in their jobs and will sometimes fight the system to maintain high standards. But overall, the system is too strong for the individual. And the system is attuned to a different set of priorities: it is too busy manipulating money to give proper attention to motivating people to produce and sell better products and services. Its eye is on the short-term profit, not on a vision of the future in which average Americans contribute more and benefit more from the fruits of competitive success. Opinion polls reveal a pattern that is not at all surprising: the majority of American jobholders believe they have little incentive to work to greater effect than they are now doing — and they do not do so.[1] The result is a wide range of American products of mediocre quality, available at high costs with indifferent service.

The shift from a low-discretion to a high-discretion workplace is one whose implications policy makers have not yet absorbed. The fact is that Japan has bested the United States on precisely those aspects of the economy that individuals now control in a high-discretion workplace: product quality, efficient costs, commitment of service, and so forth. Curiously, even though American policy makers sometimes acknowledge this fact, when it comes to remedies they fall back on their preferred technical solutions. We do not belittle these: nothing urged here should be taken to imply that macroeconomic policies are unimportant. However, we *are* arguing that they are secondary compared to improving American product quality and value.

With sound macroeconomic policies, a weaker dollar will lower the price of American products in foreign markets and an aggressive trade policy will open the Japanese market to U.S. products (to some degree). These adjustments will help moderately. By themselves, however, they will not restore competitiveness; they do not go to the heart of the matter, which is that in many product categories, from cars to bicycles, the Japanese competitive edge is a real one, and American consumers know it. Before 1985, that edge was sharpened by such factors as an advantageous yen-dollar relationship and by skillful manipulation of barriers to U.S. trade. But the heart of the Japanese success has been competent, flexible, imaginative manufacturing of quality products.

Contrary to expectations, as the dollar weakened against

the yen (while the German mark and other currencies did not), Japanese imports of German, French, and Asian products rose appreciably, but imports from the United States did not. The Japanese will not buy American products unless they are demonstrably better, even though they are priced more attractively.

There can be only one serious and effective American response: American products and services must improve in design, features, price, and marketing. That improvement will only transpire when American industry is committed to manufacturing quality products. It is unlikely to come about if American companies decide to renew manufacturing only because "the dollar is cheap." The dollar was weak in 1971 after the dismantling of fixed foreign exchange rates. It was strong in 1975, weak in 1977, strong in 1980, and weak again in 1987. If a firm opted in and out of manufacturing on such a cycle, disaster would be inescapable. The time required to gear up means that reliance on currency exchange rates as the basis for manufacturing decisions is impossible. Manufacturing is tough trench work, requiring a long-term commitment. The Japanese demonstrate that commitment. The United States must be equally committed in good times and bad, in times of weak currency and strong currency.

================= 14 =================

From Less for Less to
More for More

WE ARE ARGUING that the answer to greater competitiveness lies in America's ability to capitalize on the growth of discretionary effort in the workplace — in knowing how to manage a high-discretion workplace in an era of rapid technological development. There is hardly any American industry, however "obsolete," where the combination of a high-discretion workplace, a shrewdly selected market niche, and a judicious use of new technology has failed to create a competitive advantage. In the highly competitive steel industry, for example, some American companies now perform well in the specialty steel market. In the burgeoning telecommunications field, market niches in software give a more competitive edge than product differences in hardware do. Even in consumer electronics, where foreign companies now dominate, some American firms are competing successfully because they have learned how to manage their human assets as well as their capital. In the years ahead the United States should be able to regain part of its market domination in

manufacturing *and* services, in high-tech *and* low-tech industries. There will be one common denominator to the successful firms: they will have learned how to adapt to a high-
discretion workplace.

The more-for-more strategy derives from a uniquely American integration of discretionary effort, niche marketing,
and technology. The goal is to mobilize the American work
force around four major elements:

1. a new conception of management (more-for-more
   management) and a set of tactics for integrating technology, training, and human resources policies in
   the workplace;
2. a restoration of emphasis on manufacturing and on
   reintegrating the manufacturing process;
3. an activist, "visible hand" role for government; and
4. a new role for organized labor, education, and other
   American institutions.

A Historical Perspective

In proposing a more-for-more strategy we mark the demise
of an implicit social contract that has dominated American
industrial life since the turn of the century. Influenced by the
scientific management doctrine of Frederick Taylor and the
early miracles of Henry Ford's assembly line, American industry discovered that productivity could be increased by
simplifying jobs. The result, as we have seen, was a low-discretion workplace where jobholders exercised little control
over product quality or the effort they put into their jobs.
The harsh discipline of the factory took a toll on the lives of
workers, most of whom were immigrants or people who had
been induced to leave the farm by the high salary offered by
factories.[1]

Worker motivation was high. That motivation, however, came not from the jobs or the work environment but from the pay: it gave workers a chance to achieve the American dream. Mass production industries that did not adopt the low-discretion system found it difficult to compete. In Detroit in the 1920s, Ford paid workers the astronomical sum of $5 per day to perform the monotonous tasks called for by the auto assembly line. Ford's marriage of assembly-line technology and high wages yielded enormous production gains, even as it discouraged personal initiative, volunteering, and sharing.

A closer look at the low-discretion workplace exposes a source of America's current economic problems. At the heart of the mass production, assembly-line system was an implicit contract between management and workers. Although managers demanded a full day's work for a full day's pay, there was no call for workers to provide emotional commitment, creativity, or entrepreneurship. Indeed, Taylor regarded such "extras" as not only unnecessary but harmful. "Any improvement the worker makes upon the orders given to him," he wrote, "is fatal to success."[2]

Since workers were hired hands, they had little say in how their jobs were structured and little stake in the company. Only managers were regarded as central to the success of the organization. If times were tough, workers could be laid off and easily replaced. The implicit social contract between manager and employee was in effect "less for less." The employer or manager gave as little to the employee as competition and economic circumstance made possible, and the employee returned only as much as was necessary to avoid dismissal.

When the American work force was largely uneducated, unskilled, and unquestioning, the system worked. But those days are gone. In the contemporary workplace, an educated work force is expanding its sphere of "discretionary effort."

This term refers to the difference between the maximum amount of effort and care that an individual potentially brings to the job and the minimum amount required to avoid being fired or penalized. In other words, discretionary effort is the portion of effort that the jobholder controls. Despite its importance, this factor has been given little attention by economists, and there is no generally accepted term for it.

In today's economy the amount of discretionary effort is being significantly increased by two major transformations. One is the "second industrial revolution" characterized by computers, sophisticated communication devices, robotics, and biotechnology. By simplifying jobs, the technology of the first industrial revolution decreased discretion in the workplace. The mechanization of work on the assembly line made it possible for an uneducated labor force to build complex products in low-discretion jobs. Remarkably, the new technology reverses the trend. The best jobs created in a high-technology, knowledge-intensive economy depend on highly skilled, well-educated, and independent-minded employees. Technology is automating the routine work; the jobholder who supervises the technology has considerable control over output.[3]

A Public Agenda Foundation study shows that by 1983, nearly half of all American jobholders (44 percent) had experienced significant technological changes in their jobs in the previous five years. Of this group, a majority reported that the new technology had enlarged the scope of their work and made it more interesting (74 percent), and over half observed that it had given them greater independence on the job (55 percent). Only 21 percent felt that new technology had made their jobs more monotonous and less interesting. For the majority, technology had worked to increase their span of autonomy and control (see Chart 50).[4]

50 Increased Worker Discretion Through Technology

Q. How in particular did these technological changes affect your current job?*

As a result of technological changes, my job

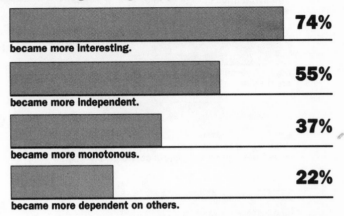

74%

became more interesting.

55%

became more independent.

37%

became more monotonous.

22%

became more dependent on others.

*Asked of those who had experienced technological change on their jobs in the past five years (44% of the total sample of members of the work force).
Source: The Public Agenda Foundation, 1982.

Attitudes toward computers and other high-tech innovations reflect the positive impact technology has on the workplace. Most people believe that in addition to increasing their discretion on the job, new technology will increase productivity and product quality and reduce job hazards (see Chart 51).

The Changing Nature of Jobs

The second transformation leading to a high-discretion workplace is a change in the nature of the paid work Americans do; away from blue-collar toward white-collar work, and,

51 Other Positive Results of Technology

Agree:

91%

The installation of high technology will enable
workers to increase their productivity.

85%

Computers can free up time for individuals to do
creative and highly productive work.

64%

With regard to high-technology production methods
in factories, the good effects outweigh the bad.

60%

Scientific and technological developments will
have a positive effect on reducing the risks of
health hazards on the job.

Sources: Harris, for Southern New England Telephone, 1983
(statements 1,2, and 4); Roper, 1985 (statement 3).

as Daniel Bell has observed, away from jobs concerned with
things toward jobs concerned with information and people.[5]

In the earlier part of the century, only one out of four
jobholders held a white-collar job; all others were employed
in low-discretion blue-collar or agricultural work. Today the
office is replacing the factory as the typical American
workplace. By the early 1980s the percentage of white-
collar workers had more than doubled (jumping to 53
percent), and managers, supervisors, and professionals now
outnumber unskilled laborers by approximately five to one.[6]

This shift increases discretion in the workplace, since professional and managerial jobs offer more discretion than unskilled jobs. Almost half of all white-collar jobholders (49 percent) say they enjoy "a great deal of freedom" in doing their job, in contrast to a third of blue-collar workers (36 percent). The Public Agenda Foundation found that only about one out of five jobholders today works in a job having little or no discretion. With more control in their hands, jobholders have the power to support or to veto demands for greater initiative, quality, service, and productivity.[7]

This marks a huge success for democratic capitalism. Socialists have always dreamed of expanding people's freedom in the workplace, but they were sure it could not be done in a capitalist economy. In fact, the U.S. economy is evolving toward ever more freedom on the job. Unfortunately, however, the growth in discretion does not pay off in quality and production gains when jobholders hold back on their commitment to the jobs.

This is just what is happening today, because the lean-and-mean strategy is not attuned to the motivations of a high-discretion workplace. The lean-and-mean approach presupposes that only managers can call the shots; the discretionary workplace spreads the responsibility down the line. The result is a serious mismatch between managerial assumptions and new realities. Most managers still operate *as if they were managing a low-discretion workplace.*

This assertion will be bitterly disputed by managers who claim to have an enlightened attitude toward their employees. But the evidence of management's failure to motivate jobholders to give their best efforts is impressive. Research findings show that vast numbers of Americans are holding back effort from their jobs.[8] Jobholders candidly admit they are giving less to their jobs than they could; for example,

- fewer than one out of four jobholders (23 percent) say they are as effective as they are capable of being and are performing to their full capacity;
- nearly half of the work force (44 percent) say they do not put a great deal of effort into their jobs over and above what is required of them; and
- a number of studies show that most workers do not believe they will be rewarded for extra effort to improve the competitiveness of their companies.

One of the most striking research findings reveals how weak the link is between pay and performance. Public Agenda Foundation research shows that almost three out of four jobholders (73 percent) see little or no connection between how good a job they do and how much they are paid; only one in five (22 percent) sees a close link (see Chart 52).

Nor do jobholders connect the well-being of their firms with their personal well-being. A U.S. Chamber of Commerce survey found that fewer than one out of ten workers (9 percent) sees herself as a beneficiary of improvements in

52 The Link Between Pay and Performance

Q. I'd like to ask you some questions about your job. Please tell me if [this phrase] describes your job fully, partly, or not at all: "A job where how much money I make depends on how good a job I do."

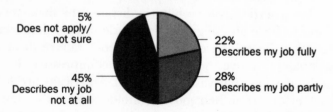

5%
Does not apply/
not sure

22%
Describes my job fully

45%
Describes my job
not at all

28%
Describes my job partly

Source: The Public Agenda Foundation, 1982.

the company's productivity. Most assume that the main ben-
eficiaries will be others — management, stockholders, consumers.[9] By contrast, the Asian Social Problems Institute
found that 93 percent of all Japanese workers believe they
will personally and directly benefit from improvements in
their employer's productivity![10]

In the past the average American had faith that hard work
pays off. But today's Americans are questioning this article
of faith. In 1968 a 58 percent majority endorsed this sentiment. Thereafter, the number of people who felt they would
be rewarded for hard work dropped sharply — to 44 percent
in 1978 and to 36 percent in 1982.[11]

It is not the case that Americans are unhappy in their
work. Research shows that job satisfaction is high. But research also shows that there is a tenuous link between job
satisfaction and job *effectiveness*. Some facets of employment,
such as having interesting work to do, enhance both satisfaction and productivity. But many important sources of worker
satisfaction are unrelated to effectiveness. Most jobholders,
for example, say that a convenient location, good fringe benefits, and low levels of rush and stress make their jobs more
satisfying, but they readily admit that these benefits do not
motivate them to work more effectively. Indeed, some attributes that make jobs more satisfying, such as having congen-
ial coworkers and supervisors, are attractive precisely because they do not require greater effort or commitment.

Other attributes of the job have the opposite effect: they
enhance productivity but diminish satisfaction. Jobholders
themselves make a sharp distinction between these two values. They see effectiveness and productivity as being enhanced by more responsibility, better chances for advancement, and a more challenging job; satisfaction is improved
by different job characteristics.

By and large, today's managers do a good job at making

jobholders feel satisfied and a poor job at motivating them to work harder and more effectively. In explaining why they do not use their discretion to improve quality and reduce costs, jobholders lay most of the blame on their managers. It is of course tempting to dismiss such criticism as routine grumbling. But that would be a mistake. In fact, jobholder perceptions of management are quite sophisticated. Most jobholders like their bosses personally and respect their dedication. Eighty-five percent say that they get along reasonably well with their supervisors, and nearly seven out of ten (69 percent) say their managers care more about getting the job done than they do about bossing people around.[12]

But jobholders feel that when it comes to knowing how to motivate people to perform more effectively, managers fall down on the job. Three quarters say that the main reason people aren't working as hard as they can is that "management doesn't know how to motivate workers." An equally large majority cite related factors such as "everyone gets the same raise regardless of how hard they work" (73 percent). (When people see that those who exert less effort get the same reward, they feel like fools.) Also, a large majority (70 percent) explain low levels of work effort by pointing out that "people don't see the end result of their work" and that "people want more of a challenge on the job" (68 percent) (see Chart 53).

Not surprisingly, jobholders resent large bonuses for managers, especially when they are taken in tough economic times when employees are being asked to hold the line. In a Roper survey, a cross section of Americans were asked what business should do with its profits. Public support for bonuses to top executives was low, whereas support for more research and development and higher worker benefits was high. Therefore, the actual deployment of business profits runs almost precisely counter to citizens' preferences (see

53 Why Jobholders Are Holding Back Effort

Q. Here are some statements that people have made about why some individuals aren't working as hard as they could. For each one, tell me whether you strongly agree, slightly agree, slightly disagree, or strongly disagree.

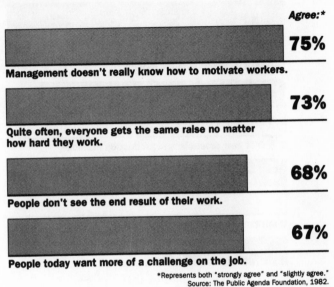

Agree:*

75%
Management doesn't really know how to motivate workers.

73%
Quite often, everyone gets the same raise no matter how hard they work.

68%
People don't see the end result of their work.

67%
People today want more of a challenge on the job.

*Represents both "strongly agree" and "slightly agree."
Source: The Public Agenda Foundation, 1982.

Chart 54). These findings will not surprise careful observers of the financial management style that has dominated American business in recent years.

Focus on Manufacturing

The high-discretion workplace has particular applicability to manufacturing. Much has been written about how America is becoming a service economy, and the service sector has certainly been the major area of growth, creating 20 million

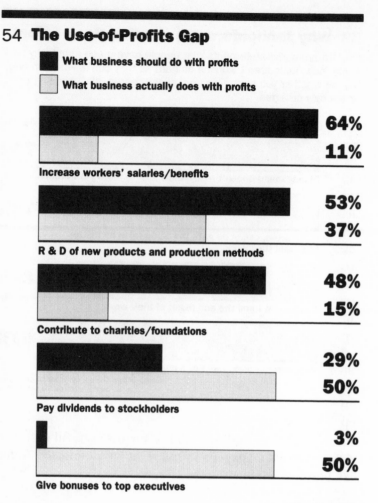

54 The Use-of-Profits Gap

■ What business should do with profits

□ What business actually does with profits

64%
11%

Increase workers' salaries/benefits

53%
37%

R & D of new products and production methods

48%
15%

Contribute to charities/foundations

29%
50%

Pay dividends to stockholders

3%
50%

Give bonuses to top executives

Source: Roper, 1983.

new jobs during the past decade. But the centerpiece of U.S. industry is still manufacturing, and it continues to grow. Manufacturing still represents more than 70 percent of merchandise exports. Because manufactured goods tend to be more exportable than services (other than financial services), this is the major arena in which the new economic battle will be fought. Manufacturing on a worldwide basis remains the focus of global competition. The United States has the resources to maintain a leading share of the world market, if Americans learn to master more-for-more techniques in the factory.

Manufacturing is in one respect like farming: it is an American tradition, to be nurtured for values over and above those associated with the bottom line. The process of manufacturing is an amalgam of ideas and technique. It requires technological and human balance. It is at once creation and development. Manufacturing does much more than produce products, growth, or wealth. It calls forth our best talent. It challenges our most fundamental facilities, and it helps us to grow. Manufacturing is a form of creativity in which Americans have excelled in the past and can excel again in the future.

A high-discretion workplace is the natural setting for flexible new manufacturing techniques and for a commitment to higher quality standards by workers who believe in a more-for-more ethic. Flexible manufacturing systems are rapidly replacing traditional assembly-line operations, which evoke Henry Ford's laconic remark, "They can have any color as long as it's black." This was not simply a mean-spirited comment; it expressed the essence of mass production, which depends on long setup times and long uninterrupted runs of unvarying models. In the new competitive environment, however, the producer cannot set the rules. The old-fashioned view that "the customer is always right" takes on new significance. Regardless of the product, if the manufacturer is to survive, he or she must be responsive to customer demand. Flexible manufacturing systems, run by highly motivated workers, serve the need. Innovative tooling designs virtually eliminate downtime. Manufacturing and design engineers work in close collaboration to increase the opportunities for product differentiation. Related facilities employ temporarily redundant workers and handle odd production tasks. Flexible manufacturing simply cannot work in a less-for-less environment: the demands on worker discretion are too great.

The conventional view is that automation, robotics, numerically controlled machines, and computer-aided manufacturing are the products of technological determinism. This view argues for the inevitability of the automated factory. It visualizes the machine directly replacing the worker. A growing body of experience demonstrates, however, that the contrary is often the case. Manufacturers in industries ranging from advanced electronics to automobiles have hastily overautomated and undertaken major capital programs that have proved excessive. In most instances management has failed to consult those who will be most affected by the new technology — the workers in the offices and factories. This viewpoint understates the role of the worker and overstates that of the machine.

Computer-controlled lathes, for example, are marvelous machines — when managed by operators who exercise supervisory judgment. The same machine that can produce superbly made parts, however, can also destroy inventory if it is not sensitively attended. The new high-technology machine tools require operator discretion and judgment if they are to justify their purchase. In a more-for-more environment, new manufacturing technology permits the work to be done with fewer workers, but their role is enlarged and their responsibilities increased. When appropriate equilibrium is achieved between the new machines and the new workers, opportunities are often created for in-house production, replacing production that was previously purchased elsewhere and thus increasing the total employment of the company.

Because the more-for-more environment encourages respect for the product, apathy is replaced by enthusiasm, and a concern for quality is nourished. The impulse to learn more about the machine and its maintenance provokes respect for the technology, and a heightened level of self-esteem and personal identification with the product follows.

In summary, the shift from a low- to a high-discretion workplace in both the office and the factory has caught American management unprepared. Neither the old engineer-boss managerial style nor the new lean-and-mean financial style is geared to a high-discretion workplace. Both fail to tap the greatest resource America enjoys: the energies, skills, and commitment of its people.

Consensus I — Political

THE CENTRAL QUESTION we pose in this book is stated in the Introduction: How can the nation reach consensus on how best to compete with the Soviet Union in the military and political sphere and with Japan and other trade competitors? In Part I we hypothesized that the best way to achieve consensus about U.S.-Soviet competition is to develop a policy grounded in the public's values. For voters to move from mass opinion to true public judgment, they must focus on concrete alternatives to expert-initiated policies; otherwise the hard work of resolving the underlying clashes of values will be blocked. In Part I we sketched the broad features of a common security policy and showed how it is anchored in the public's most fundamental values.

We are now ready to tackle the second half of the question: how to reach consensus on competing with Japan and other nations. As in Part I, we propose a policy grounded in the people's own values — more for more. At this point, however, we run up against a complication. A consensus on economic competitiveness demands more from the public than one on U.S.-Soviet competition does. On that issue people are involved exclusively as voters. But in the implementation of a competitive strategy, more than voter acquiescence is needed. People are engaged as voters and as workers, managers, savers, and consumers. Here the American people perform as players — and essential ones.

In effect, therefore, two different forms of consensus are needed for economic competitiveness: *political* consensus to support government policy at the national and state levels, and *workplace* consensus to support the activity of firms at the microeconomic level. The two are related, but they are distinct from each other. It is easy to imagine people voting for a right-minded policy for the government to pursue without being motivated to give more personally to their jobs. Different values are involved: political consensus calls on values such as the desire of consumers for quality products at reasonable prices and the will to win against international competitors, whereas workplace consensus calls on values such as pride of work and personal fulfillment on the job. In this chapter and the next we sketch the broad features of these two forms of consensus.

Resolving the Clash of Values

The first requirement of a new political consensus is that it pass the values test. As we have seen, the penalty suffered by any policy that fails to conform to *all* of the people's relevant values is public volatility. In Chapter 13 we showed that protectionism fails the values test in that it appeals to some of the public's values (the desire to safeguard jobs and certain aspects of fairness) but neglects others (for example, consumer choice and the will to win).

Keeping faith with all the people's basic values is difficult to do, because these values harbor a major conflict, described in Chapter 13 as the clash between market and communal values. One of the central political questions of our era is how the public will resolve this conflict. In the future, will the public give priority to market values? Or will it pursue communal values at the expense of market values, as Britain and the Scandinavian countries did in the 1960s and 1970s? Or will it strike a balance between the two?

We have seen that regarding U.S.-Soviet relations, the public has opted for a balanced treatment of the threats of nuclear war and Soviet expansionism. Regarding economic competitiveness, however, our analysis suggests that the public leans toward giving market values the higher priority — without neglecting the communal values, of course. This is not double talk: in practical terms, there is a profound difference between policies that give equal priority to both sets of values and policies that take communal values into account but do not give them the same priority as market values.

The policies of Reagan conservatism clearly favor market values. How, then, will a more-for-more consensus be different? Reagan conservatism takes a principled stand against active government protection of communal values. The more-for-more strategy proposes an aggressive promarket stance supported by active government involvement in communal values. If competition and free trade are to prevail, we must make provisions to ease the hurt to those who become victims through no fault of their own.

Americans are very ambivalent about competition from abroad, especially when it is seen as harming the U.S. economy. Most people recognize that competition between companies (both domestic and international) brings both benefits and drawbacks. People realize that not all companies can be winners: an overwhelming majority of Americans (90 percent) acknowledge that whenever there is free competition, some companies are bound to go out of business.[1] But they also recognize that competition produces higher-quality products and services at lower prices. The public is firmly in favor of competition, but it also supports some cushioning against the "creative destructiveness" of market forces.

If possible, we must guard against direct collision between communal and market values; neither extreme can win politically. In the post-Reagan era, a conservative free-market ideology that violates communal values will be stopped in its tracks through the political process. A liberal ideology that violates market values or advocates an industrial policy that picks winners will be torn apart by those who are officially designated as losers, on the grounds of unfairness and with the full support of the electorate. A policy that pits communal values directly against market values or vice versa may appear to have public support, but under pressure that support will prove as treacherous as quicksand.

It is worth emphasizing again that Americans are not demanding that communal and market values receive equal weight. Most Americans are pragmatic and realistic. They know that competing with Japan is rough work and that sacrifices will be needed. They are willing to tip the balance in favor of market values. But they insist that the rules be fair and that the victims be helped. It is this insistence that dictates a large and positive role for government, at the same time that the private enterprise system is left free to respond to the challenge.

The Expert—Public Gap

A strategy that gives market values priority but also recognizes the claims of communal values will help to close the gap between the experts and the public and thus move toward political consensus. A Gallup poll for the Chicago Council on

Foreign Affairs (Oct.-Nov. 1986) shows just how wide that gap is. Policy makers don't like tariffs and are not greatly concerned about the threat to American jobs; the public holds the opposite view. Like other polls (see Chapter 12), this one found a two-thirds majority of the public favoring protective tariffs (66 percent), whereas fewer than half that number of policy makers believe that tariffs are necessary (31 percent). Conversely, an overwhelming 79 percent of the public, in contrast to a minority of policy makers (44 percent), regard protecting American jobs as vitally important.[2]

These differences in values are large and important, but they do not stand in the way of public consensus nearly as much as the splitting of elites into liberal and conservative camps. It is very difficult for the public to form a stable judgment when the leadership is divided. Fortunately for the country, there has been recent progress on this front. The process of reconciling the experts' ideological differences is advancing rapidly. This constructive trend has occurred out of sight of the public, and it illustrates a peculiar feature of the American political scene that is worth remarking on.

There exists in the nation an informal institution, sometimes called the invisible university, made up of the countless seminars, conferences, meetings, discussion groups, workshops, institutes, and so forth in which policy makers in business, government, labor, and education meet with each other to hear the views of leading experts. Of all the topics covered in the invisible university, the future of the U.S. economy receives the most attention.

The tone of these private discussions contrasts with the acrimony of public debate: it is civil, undogmatic, nonconfrontational. Though billed as informational, these meetings often convey facts and figures as a secondary role. Their major purpose is to foster problem solving and learning to see old problems in fresh ways.

The cumulative effect of countless meetings of the invisible university has had an impact on the competitiveness debate. From the mid-1970s to the mid-1980s, the debate revolved mainly around the free market versus industrial policy. By the mid-1980s the participants had come to realize that the terms of this debate were irrelevant to the real issues. The free market advocates of the Reagan Administration found themselves forced to take governmental actions to restrict imports and raise tariffs, which in theory they opposed. The industrial policy advocates came to see the disadvantages of requiring government to make decisions that properly have to be made in response to market conditions.

Ever so slowly, the experts began to realize that the debate between free market and industrial policy was placing too much emphasis on government — as if government decision making were the decisive factor in the solution. The assumption behind the free market position was that if government interference could be reduced, the *magic of the free market* would solve the problem of competitiveness. The assumption behind the industrial policy position was that if government involvement could be increased, the *magic of government* would solve the problem. There are still partisans who cleave to these positions. But the centrist majority has come to realize that the role of government, although important, is not decisive: what the government does or fails to do will not by itself determine whether this country restores its competitiveness in world markets.

This insight has caused the semantics of the debate to change. In about the middle of the 1980s, policy makers began to label the problem as "the competitiveness issue" rather than "the industrial policy debate." The term quickly became a buzz word, for Republicans and Democrats, liberals and conservatives. On the surface this seems an almost trivial change. But the change goes far deeper than semantics. The shift in phraseology signals a new readiness to discuss the problem of declining U.S. competitiveness in nonideological terms. Pragmatic conservatives are ready to suspend some of their prejudices against using the "visible hand" of government where needed to improve competitiveness, and pragmatic liberals are ready to give greater support to private initiatives and free market forces (with government playing a lesser role).

This is a major shift — a helpful and liberating change in the terms of the debate. The ability of liberals and conservatives to find an ideological meeting ground narrows the gap between policy makers and the public. In the political debate, conservatives will push for adherence to market values and liberals will call for attention to communal values. With the two sides talking to each other instead of haranguing each other, it should be possible to devise a new role for government that keeps faith with the public's values of fairness, preserving consumer choice, maximizing job opportunities, and winning the economic competition.

The Role of Government
in a Political Consensus

What role might government play in a more-for-more policy? The liberal policies of Lyndon Johnson's Great Society assigned a central role to government, giving priority to communal values. Reagan conservatism swung the pendulum in the opposite direction, promoting a new form of Social Darwinism in which government has been discouraged from interfering with the "laws" of the market, irrespective of the human consequences. (In practice, the rich and powerful have been protected; the poor and the weak have not.) In the post-Reagan era, it is likely that a more positive role for government will be reconstituted, but that it will be in keeping with the more-for-more principle of giving priority to market values (which means that government's role, although important, will be secondary to that of the private sector).

Most Americans prefer the government to be active in two roles: helping the private sector as facilitator and catalyst, and insuring that communal values do not get trampled. These two roles constitute the public's conception of the national interest. Regarding the first role, an impressive majority of the people (84 percent) believe that government should make an effort "to help American business become more competitive in foreign markets." Only 12 percent think that government should play no role at all.[3] Regarding specific proposals for government action,

- 68 percent of Americans agree that the federal government should increase "by a sizable amount" the money it gives to colleges and universities for basic scientific and technological research"[4];
- 83 percent feel that the government "should encourage companies to work together to develop high-technology products to enable American companies to compete better against the Japanese"[5]; and
- 81 percent believe that government should play an active role in supporting "research and development in high technology."[6]

As government shifts from its regulatory and welfare-state role of the 1960s and 1970s to a supportive role for industry, it recognizes that the main player in revitalizing American competitiveness must be a private sector as free as possible from regulations and constraints. But the public sector helps to create the conditions that will assist companies to become more competitive and to insure that the communal values in the national interest are well represented. The conservative assumption that the sum of all individual market decisions will automatically serve the national interest (the "invisible hand") is not borne out by experience. Many business decisions give too much weight to short-term considerations whose effect may be to undercut that interest (for instance, decisions to produce in other nations, to skimp on research and development, to neglect the skill level of the work force, and to sacrifice other values important to the community).

The more-for-more strategy calls for a return to the concept of a mixed economy, though the proposed mix of public and private activities will be different from what it was in the past. We propose a *visible hand* strategy that calls for an activist, but not coercive, role for government. In effect government says to the private sector, "There is no mandatory direction from government. Within the law, you are free to make your business decisions as narrowly or broadly as you wish. If, however, you are willing to take into account the national interest as the public has identified it, the government is prepared to offer you certain advantages."

One possible mechanism might be a National Interest Board. Such an entity would include senior representatives from Congress and the White House. Through the board, government would join management and labor in forging voluntary national interest contracts through which government would offer industries various forms of assistance in exchange for policies that advance important national objectives in job creation, employment security, training, technology development, and international competitiveness.

National interest contracts would engage all the critical institutions: government, industry, unions, and schools. They would fully respect collective bargaining agreements. They would establish the terms of undertakings to support full employment, build new manufacturing facilities in the United States, create new jobs, develop programs for training and education as an integral part of the working day, and foster worker participation in decision making.

The board would prod government to fund training schools and to permit firms to establish their own depreciation schedules for new plants and equipment (as long as the chosen schedule was employed in both the firm's public reports and its tax reports). It would also press the Justice Department to serve as counselor in developing cooperative plans that would not violate antitrust law.

Through the board, government would promote and participate in agreements sector by sector, firm by firm, community by community, in which each would undertake shared commitments to the national interest. Each agreement would be voluntary, and the initiative would be taken by the industrial sector. Each agreement would have to demonstrate that it was in the national interest, and each would be monitored on an ongoing basis to insure full implementation. For example, a firm might bargain to generate a particular level of employment in exchange for training contributions by the local university, revised shop rules by the union, and relaxed depreciation schedules and technological assistance from the government. The ultimate question would always be "Does it advance the national interest?"

Among communal values, employment security is of paramount importance to most working people. Fear of job loss can be paralyzing. If we seek an environment in which workers give their all, it must include some credible underpinning of employment security. Managers may well recognize the long-term value of this but fear the short-term wrath of investors. National interest agreements could help pave the way for acceptance of the necessary compromises.

But employment security that is not rooted in real work at healthy firms will not do. If we were to shield half a million jobs in protectionist ways, we would spend in the range of

$50 billion annually. In 1980 the Federal Trade Commission reported that the costs to the country for each job protected by tariff or quota was well in excess of $100,000. Similarly, when the Departments of Commerce and Labor reviewed the costs of Trade Adjustment Assistance for 1980, they calculated that the direct, out-of-pocket costs to the Treasury exceeded $100,000 for every job given assistance in response to unfair foreign trade practices. In 1982 the Congressional Budget Office reported that during 1980 there had been half a million applications for Trade Adjustment Assistance, but only 3 percent of the applicants were actually placed in new jobs. At a program cost of $1.7 billion for the year, the cost per placement was well in excess of $100,000.[7] Thus, with respect to tariffs and quotas, the costs of which are essentially hidden in the higher product costs to the consumer for each protected job, and in the case of Trade Adjustment Assistance, where the cost is direct, we see that each protected job has cost the nation directly or indirectly in excess of $100,000 per year.

One of the biggest stumbling blocks to consensus would be removed if the nation developed a more practical approach to protecting job security in an equitable way consistent with consensus and at a fraction of the cost of tariff-driven strategies. One possible method might involve a quid pro quo between industry and the National Interest Board. A company or group of companies in an industry (competing for a market) or in a geographic area (competing for the same labor pool) would meet with the National Interest Board to design a proposal to improve employment security. The term would be a minimum of one year. The board would negotiate the terms of a national interest contract that would calculate the cost of the program and divide it equitably among the parties through a tax credit equal to a maximum of 50 percent of the incremental cost — that is, the cost each firm would experience above an agreed-upon base or standard. The program might include the creation of a separate company or school so that temporarily redundant people would have constructive work to do and/or receive on-site training while employed. Better yet, all employees might participate, which would fractionally reduce the total number of hours worked by everyone in the company, spread the work equitably, and create no separated class of workers.

Our proposal of national interest contracts and a National Interest Board suggests a mechanism for generating the appropriate mix between market and communal values. That mix is an essential precondition to political consensus.

Consensus II — The Workplace

POLITICAL CONSENSUS gives priority to market values without scanting communal ones. In practice, this means political support for free trade rather than protectionism, for open markets, for vigorous competition, and for a cautious use of regulation as a mechanism of control. It also means finding new ways to preserve employment. And it means an active role for government in giving communal values their due and in assisting American industry to compete more effectively.

Workplace consensus is different. The need in this case is for people to give more than their vote: nothing less than a major commitment is called for, and from many sources — the work force, management, labor, government, education, and the community at large. We have described this commitment as a new social contract in the workplace, summarized as "more for more." Its premise is that there is no quick fix or short cut to increased American competitiveness. What is needed instead is a return to the fundamentals: giving customers top quality at reasonable prices in competition with the highly motivated, skilled, intelligent, ambitious Asians. In practical terms, this means a heavy reliance on people and technology, in contrast to the current fashion of relying primarily on capital and neglecting the "people factor."

Given the values of the American people, the nation is ready for a new social contract — *if* it is implemented skillfully and fairly. But this is a big "if." The transition from Wall Street's fixation on short-term profits and gimmicky changes in corporate structure will not be easy to make, although market panics and hard times have the effect of forcing change. Fortunately, some companies and individuals (including leaders in labor, education, and state government) are moving rapidly in the right direction.

In this chapter we summarize how the various parts fit together to form a consensus in support of the more-for-more social contract of the future. It is useful to visualize a hexagon linking jobholders in an active network with management, organized labor, education, community, and government (see Chart 55). The hexagon is essentially a structure of mutual support, promoting job creation and elevated standards of living, skill and education, leading in turn to greater economic security and competitiveness.

The crucible is the workplace. This is where the shared and differing values and roles of the players meet and can be forged into a live, dynamic process. It is the one setting that generates equilibrium among the participants in the hexagon. It is in the workplace that

- *management* can forge policies that motivate jobholders to use their discretionary effort to fullest competitive effect;
- *trade unions* can become again a major force for the growth and security of workers, through participation in the development of the firm;

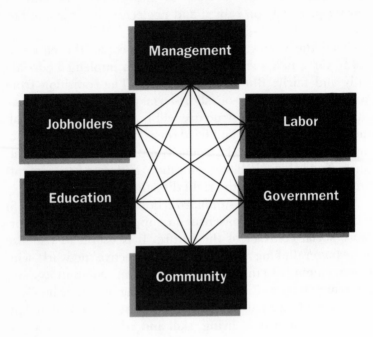

- *education* can contribute more effectively to the development of the nation's human resources;
- *government* can provide new leadership as the principal facilitator of the process; and
- *the community* can actively realize shared values and responsibilities.

There is no easy path to the high-discretion, more-for-more workplace. Achieving it will be a tough, grinding, long-term development — a three-stage hierarchy:

1. The more-for-more workplace can promise real success only if at the outset there is a recognized need for change. The change can originate either with management or with jobholders. In either event it requires long, patient persuasion of others, and realization that serious change comes slowly.

2. The second stage is the period of experimentation — of trial and error, evaluation and feedback. It is the stage during which practices aimed at generating mutual dependence and trust are developed. This is the period of hard-fought experience, not of glib slogans or premature programs.

3. Stage three is not likely to be reached in less than three to five years. But then, as managers and jobholders come to support each other, profit sharing, employee stock ownership plans (ESOPs), and other such plans can be made to work. The third stage is one in which the energy, hard work, and emotional investment of the first two stages are translated into a healthy and enduring system. It is consensus achieved.

The Jobholders

The most important change in the work force since the end of World War II has been the emergence of the baby-boom generation. Over 74 million Americans were born in the eighteen-year period between 1946 and 1964.[1] Today these people constitute about half of the working-age population of the United States.[2] The older members of this cohort, now fortyish, are moving into the most productive years of their working lives. Their impact on the workplace is virtually doubled by the fact that women as well as men are now working for pay and plan to continue to do so in the future. Fewer than one woman in four has chosen to be a full-time home-maker, and more than two thirds of all baby-boom women are either working at paid jobs or looking for paid work.[3] Most baby-boom parents of young children are working, either in dual-earner families or single-parent families.

The baby-boom generation is the best-educated group ever to enter the American workplace. Nearly half (46 percent) have completed one year of college, compared to about 29 percent of those who were born before 1946, and more than five million baby-boomers are still in school.[4] These younger and better-educated jobholders require more from jobs than their parents did. They bring to the workplace a new value system, which emphasizes the expressive side of life.

In the 1960s and early 1970s, young Americans believed they could fulfill their need for self-expression through leisure — in the mountains, travel, sports, sexuality, personal relations, and drugs. They saw the workplace as the trap that had ensnared their fathers in a nose-to-the-grindstone way of life they desperately wanted to escape. This rejection of the workplace made a strong impression on managers, and led them to underestimate the productive potential of the baby-boom generation.[5]

Then, in the 1980s, baby-boomers made a momentous discovery. Work rather than leisure could give them what they were looking for: an outlet for self-expression as well as material rewards. Nearly two thirds of Americans between thirty and forty years of age say that they place more emphasis on "pursuing a satisfactory career" than their parents did. Today these people look to their jobs to satisfy a variety of important values: making a living, being independent (especially for women), achieving success, developing new skills, testing themselves competitively against others, exploring new experiences, enjoying the companionship of others, doing interesting things, making a lot of money, and conquering new worlds. It is not surprising that a large majority of young Americans (75 percent) say that they would *not* like to see our society de-emphasize hard work.

The major effect of the new expressive values on the workplace has been to transform the meaning of the work ethic. The roots of the old meaning go far back in Western history. The Greek word for work is *ponos*, which also means "pain." Pain, sacrifice, and drudgery have been associated with work throughout history. The Protestant work ethic assumed that pain and sacrifice are inherent in work, and maintained that work is a sacrifice that has the stamp of moral worthiness. In principle, hard work is to be rewarded later, postponed gratification being the essence of the Protestant idea.

Today work is no longer synonymous with pain, sacrifice, and postponement. Instead it is seen as good in itself — an activity in which individuals become themselves. An overwhelming majority of Americans (87 percent) say that it is very important to them that they enjoy their work.[6] When asked what makes for the "good life," three out of five (61 percent) say, "A job that is interesting."[7]

This new focus is shaping a new kind of work ethic. Instead of emphasizing sacrifice, the ethic now stresses skill, challenge, autonomy, recognition, and the quality of work produced, because the product of an individual's work is an intimate expression of the self. Work is once again valued for something beyond mere commercial transaction. In the Public Agenda Foundation's research, more than half of all jobholders (52 percent) described themselves as having "an inner need to do the best job possible regardless of pay," and an additional 21 percent acknowledged positive value in their work while looking to their nonworking lives for their greatest personal satisfaction. Only 26 percent saw work as nothing but a commercial transaction or as one of life's unpleasant necessities (a bumper sticker put this sentiment succinctly: "Work sucks, but I need the bucks") (see Chart 56).

Q. Here are four persons talking about work. Which one of the four do you think comes closest to your own view?

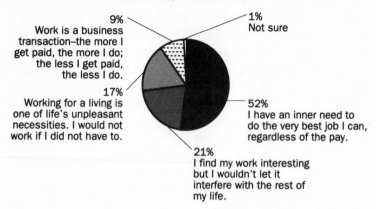

9%
Work is a business transaction–the more I get paid, the more I do; the less I get paid, the less I do.

1%
Not sure

17%
Working for a living is one of life's unpleasant necessities. I would not work if I did not have to.

52%
I have an inner need to do the very best job I can, regardless of the pay.

21%
I find my work interesting but I wouldn't let it interfere with the rest of my life.

Source: The Public Agenda Foundation, 1982.

This new work ethic has much broader support in the United States than in other industrialized democracies such as the United Kingdom, where only 17 percent of jobholders express "an inner need to do the best job possible regardless of pay."[8]

The University of Minnesota's Jeylan Mortimer, Michael Finch, and Geoffrey Maruyama found that autonomy on the job is the single strongest determinant of job satisfaction, even more than income. It is true that people who earn high incomes are usually satisfied with their work, but they are also the people who enjoy the highest levels of autonomy. These researchers learned that even people in lower-paying jobs are happy with them, provided they have real autonomy. The study showed that autonomy is especially important to younger workers.[9] What young Americans most crave is to feel themselves to be "owners," "holders," "players," "participants" — in a word, stakeholders.

Self-expression has transformed what it means to be a stakeholder. In the 1950s Americans felt that they held a stake in life when they married, raised a family, owned a home and car, and became members of the community. These values remain important. But in addition, Americans in the 1980s define holding a stake in terms of participation on the job. They want to become owners or part owners of a business, to be included in a profit-sharing plan, to receive merit pay, or to invest in a house or condo. Most young Americans do not crave great economic power; their aspirations are grounded in practicality. What they do crave is more control over their work: more autonomy, more opportunity to shape the decisions that affect their jobs, and more immediate, proportionate rewards when they do a good job.

Not surprisingly, then, the baby-boom generation has enthusiastically embraced entrepreneurship. In 1984 twice as many businesses were formed in the United States (600,000) as a decade earlier, many by people in this age group. And the young entrepreneurs have shown themselves willing to work incredibly hard — as much as sixty, seventy, or eighty hours a week — if their jobs fulfill their dual goals of expressive *and* conventional success.

In sum, the work ethic in the United States has not been abandoned; it has changed. In its transformed state it leads to a high-discretion workplace where the commitment and entrepreneurship of the work force are indispensable to future competitiveness.

The Managers

What kind of manager can best elicit the energy and commitment of this new breed of American jobholder? The current style of financial management is exactly the opposite of what is needed.

Styles of management have changed several times in the past eighty years. The early part of the century featured managers with production and engineering backgrounds — people comfortable on the shop floor. The era after World War II featured managers with a marketing orientation, who were comfortable with fashioning products to meet consumer needs in mass markets. In recent years financial managers have graduated to the command positions.

Unfortunately, most financial managers are ill-suited to a more-for-more strategy, which requires them to earn commitment and loyalty from others. They are more comfortable with managing money than people, and they characteristically prefer to keep control in their own hands rather than share it. Moreover, their preoccupation with the financial side of business is often so one-sided that they neglect the high standards of product and customer service required in the new competitive climate.

Admittedly, managing people is more difficult than managing money — and the more-for-more managerial style is not easy to grasp. Its subtleties require experience and learning. Consider, for example, the difficulties of implementing something as simple as profit sharing. The concept is implicit in the more-for-more social contract, yet there are pitfalls that managers must guard against. One serious limitation of traditional profit-sharing plans is that bottom-line profit is not directly connected to the performance of the manufacturing employees. If they do a good job at producing an ill-conceived product, there will be no profit to share. Although asking jobholders to share financial risks with the company may be appropriate as a final goal, it is rarely a sound first step, especially if mutual trust has not been built.

In many firms profit sharing is introduced during periods of high profitability. After several years participants come to regard a share of the profits as a fixed part of their compensation, and they are confused and disappointed when profits (and, as a result, their bonuses) diminish or disappear. Without understanding how the system really works, and with no basis for confidence and trust in management, employees have little alternative to disenchantment and anger. When prematurely introduced, profit-sharing plans are almost certain to disappoint.

A "cost savings sharing" plan may be a better first or second step. Cost savings sharing (CSS) is built on the premise that reasonable cost estimates can be agreed on for every function. If the plant produces the product or function at a cost below the standard, the company will benefit and should share the results with those who create them. A portion of the sharing is set aside for the support functions (warehousing, receiving, shipping, inspection, credits, collections, and so on), so that everyone in the plant — blue-, gray-, and white-collar — will participate. The plan acknowledges the interdependence of all participants and actively encourages it.

CSS establishes a standard and rewards those who work together to exceed that standard. It is essentially independent of bottom-line profit or loss, because if the company is operating unprofitably, the losses are greater in the absence of the plan. CSS is a good starting place for more-for-more management, because it eliminates some of the problems associated with profit sharing and concentrates on the part of the job that an employee can affect directly.

Another perplexing problem for management is how to introduce new technology in ways that will enhance commitment, not undercut it. (We use the term *technology* to include working methods and product designs as well as hardware such as computers, robots, and communications systems.) The manager's dilemma is easy to state: the main incentive for introducing new technology is to do the job better and at less cost. Reducing the labor component and doing the job impeccably the first time is the key. But if the effect of technological change is to lay off workers, jobholders are faced with a conflict of interest. If they accept the new technology, they hurt themselves.

This conflict has always been present, but in a high-discretion workplace it takes on new urgency. Under high-discretion conditions, jobholders have more power to make or break the success of the technology, and unless they have a clear stake in its success, they will not be fully committed to support it.

In the second stage of the more-for-more strategy, workers and managers must share a common interest in the new technology. This requires managers to couple work-saving technology with a concern for the employment security of those who will be most directly affected. The fundamental principle for companies to accept is that technology must not cause job loss. This conflicts directly with any impulse to use technology simply to eliminate jobs. If jobholders are expected to give more, in terms of a committed and creative response to the introduction of the technology, they must be offered more — in this case, an assurance that they will not suffer economic hardship and that they will have more opportunity to improve their skills and roles.

A commitment to greater employment security raises serious problems for most companies. Since product demand is not infinite, highly productive jobholders may well run out of work. One way to cope with this is to form a school on the plant grounds. Whenever people complete their standard day's work, they are encouraged to attend classes, which ideally will be continuously available. Classes should offer them the opportunity to improve their level of competence or acquire new skills, but should not be limited to immediately relevant work skills. Classes in health, language, auto repair, and statistical quality control might be included.

Because people working in a plant rarely, if ever, have an

opportunity to see the final product of their labor, one course might introduce them to other parts of the process and teach them how the system as a whole works. Several benefits would follow. First, giving employees a clear picture of their contribution to the overall product strengthens the belief that what they do is important. Further, some workers will learn that they are good at other parts of the system, including sales and customer service, which will open new opportunities for individuals. There might also be a course in the arithmetic of business, which would encourage employees to understand how pricing and costing are done and how profits or losses are generated. Such a course would reflect management's conviction that the informed worker is more likely to make a long-term commitment to the firm.

In sum, a series of programs that are integral with the work, that are relatively easy to understand and retain, and that over time build trust and a proprietary sense become the basis of a permanent and sophisticated system.

Cost savings sharing and job security and training programs are first steps in a process that culminates in developing a true profit-sharing plan. When jobholders develop trust and confidence in management, they can fairly be expected to share the defeats as well as the victories. When a truly shared responsibility has developed, profit sharing and equal participation become practical.

Management in a more-for-more workplace has been given different names by various people. Jack MacAllister, chairman of US WEST, calls it "strategic management," in contrast to the "control management" style of the Bell Telephone system in which he was trained.[10] MacAllister states that his main job is "to make other people into heroes." He sees himself as a resource to help others accomplish their objective within the framework of an overall strategy, rather than as an all-powerful, distant figure who moves assets —

capital, people, technology, plant, and equipment — around a giant checkerboard. He refers to the tendency of his former employer, AT&T, to "oversteer" its staff, and speaks of management's preoccupation with the need to maintain control almost for its own sake. MacAllister rejects this "control management" in favor of working with colleagues to shape strategic objectives and then supporting them as they develop the tactics to accomplish those goals. MacAllister says that he runs a ranch-style organization — a one-level affair, without the vertical management structure common to hierarchical companies.

One of us (Sidney Harman) has described the new style as "prismatic management," because the manager acts as a prismatic lens, refracting the various elements of a business so that they converge on a single focused goal. In this style of management, corporate decisions are truly corporate, the product of joint action. The manager is the instrument rather than the commander.

Today's ideal manager is much more likely to be a generalist than a specialist, or better still, a generalist developed from a specialist. He or she may have begun in production or marketing but has learned to respect other disciplines. He knows that finance, financial evaluations, and reporting are the interpreting means of industry, not its ends. His contribution is measured not in terms of the growth of his own power but in the development of others. Thinking holistically and encouraging such thinking in others is his distinction.

Bernard Schwartz, chief executive officer of Loral, a major defense electronics company, practices the more-for-more policy in a different fashion. He recognized that the scientists and engineers on whose commitment the success of his company ultimately depends were not receiving the same high levels of rewards as managers with traditional business skills. He therefore developed ingenious incentive programs to close the gap and to insure that those directly responsible for the quality of the product would receive rewards commensurate with their performance.

More-for-more managers will of course differ in style. Some are more articulate than others; some are outgoing, others are reserved. But all reveal common characteristics. Their working process is organic, horizontal, and collegial rather than mechanical, vertical, and commanding. Their commitment to the undertaking is long-term. They seek opportunities for growth, personal development, and renewal for others.

Government

Our proposals for a more-for-more workplace focus on microeconomic policy — on how to support the millions of individual firms on the front line of the competitive battle. To achieve this support, government has an indispensable role to play as facilitator and catalyst.

A little-known government program that operated on behalf of the shoe industry in the late 1970s illustrates one way to do this. In 1966 the shoe industry began to experience industry-wide decline. In 1977 it petitioned the Carter Administration for tariff protection, which the administration rejected. Instead, the government agreed to temporary, orderly marketing agreements with Taiwan and Korea, where the competition in shoe production was strong. The quid pro quo was an agreement that domestic shoe manufacturers would participate in an experimental program called the Footwear Industry Revitalization Program.

Initially the plan was met with skepticism from industry representatives. They were convinced that government had little to offer. Nonetheless, the Commerce Department embarked on a three-year plan with a total budget of $56 million. (Most was used for low-interest loans, and most of the loaned money was repaid.) It began by organizing working teams drawn from both government and the private sector, typically including an engineering-production specialist, an accounting specialist, and a marketing counselor. The teams visited most of the distressed firms and held seminars to analyze production methods, marketing strategies, and cost-accounting practices on a firm-by-firm basis. The anti-trust division of the Department of Justice joined the preliminary meetings to anticipate violations, instead of playing the traditional role of reacting to violations after they occur.

It quickly became apparent that assistance was needed at virtually every firm. Some producers were making good products but had little conception of cost controls or marketing; others had excellent cost mechanisms but no marketing skills. Few managements had given thought to nonadversarial, cooperative, more-for-more arrangements with their employees.

Once it became clear that government was taking a businesslike, "hands-on" approach rather than a legalistic, regulatory one, industry resistance evaporated, with positive results. Firms that had operated with no costing systems or obsolete ones introduced new systems, in the realization that they could not compete without detailed knowledge of their costs. Other firms needed production assistance and accepted it eagerly. Still others welcomed help in styling and marketing. A Footwear Center was established to stimulate new technology and to provide product and materials testing. An export program was initiated in an industry where there had been virtually no previous activity.

After eighteen months of the program, dozens of firms

were committed to the new working arrangement with government, and the eleven-year decline in the industry was arrested. Despite heavy foreign competition and deft circumvention of the orderly marketing agreements by Korea and Taiwan, the industry made progress on many fronts. This was not because of government protection, but because of economic vigor on the part of managers and workers, assisted by skilled government aides.

In 1981 the Reagan Administration discontinued the program, stating that it had done its job. The industry again fell into decline and has become widely identified as a symbol of America's loss of traditional industries. But some shoe firms continue to be successful, and some trace their success to the program.

It should come as no surprise that the industry fell into old habits when the catalyst withdrew. The effort had been in place for only three years, in a trade where much of the management had been moribund for decades. The habit of seeking relief from government quickly overwhelmed the initiative toward self-sufficiency. Seeking tariff barriers against competitors proved all too seductive and all too consistent with the industry's former practice of lobbying. After all, the shoe industry could claim it was losing jobs in thirty-two states, and that appeal helped to rally sixty-four senators to its aid.

It is easy to criticize managers who seek the easy way out. But we cannot readily write off the several hundred thousand workers who have spent their lives in American shoe plants, or the well-run companies that did learn to compete effectively even in adverse conditions. Those companies, including Timberland, Amwelt, Stride-Rite, and others, were determined to find their own market niches. They operate efficiently and respect their customers and the people who work their factories, and they have continued to progress.

There are a number of useful conclusions to be drawn from the shoe industry's experience.

- The country does not need to abandon older, middle-sized industries in the conviction that technology has passed them by. In many cases these medium-to-small regional manufacturers make a contribution to the economy of an area, and they also provide the principal employment. When a local shoe manufacturer goes, a town may be threatened with extinction. Precipitate decisions to write such businesses off may well prove both cruel and unnecessary.
- Government has the resources to help such industries. Moreover, these are underwritten by the taxes of the firms and people whom they might well serve.
- Many industrialists believe that government itself is the problem. They fear government incompetence. Practical, nonbureaucratic programs can enhance the citizens' image of government.
- Successful programs can do much to energize government. Many talented civil servants are frustrated in their wish to make a serious contribution to the nation. An involved, to-the-point style is precisely what is needed to stimulate both sides of the government-industry partnership.
- Such programs may not save all or even a majority of firms in a troubled industry, but they can greatly improve the odds.

A staggering amount of technical, statistical, demographic, and scientific information has been developed during the past decades in various departments of the federal government. Unfortunately, no mechanism exists to make it readily available to industry and academia. To strengthen U.S. competitiveness, this information should be made available to the companies that need it. Particular attention should be given to the needs of small and medium-sized businesses, which have less access to the information than the country's largest industrial firms. Smaller firms, which have been responsible for most of the growth and job creation the country has recently experienced, are much less able to "work" the government bureaucracies or to generate quantities of information for themselves.

Unions

The more-for-more strategy calls for a new role for organized labor. Ironically, the trade union movement has had the good fortune of suffering serious reverses in recent years. Sometimes rebuffs and failure are the only way to get rid of obsolete habits of mind. Trade unions are highly conservative institutions: they like to do things the way they have in the past. But the future will require a changed labor movement, and undoubtedly the reversals of recent years have encouraged the unions to consider new approaches.

Beyond a changed trade union movement, the future will depend to a great extent on how effectively organized labor functions. Without the unions, there is no effective bargaining representation; it is left to management to determine what is fair. Generally, managements of companies change more frequently than managements of unions, and there is no assurance that new managers will endorse the more-for-more approach. It is the unions that may offer the best promise of continuity.

In the more-for-more strategy, organized labor has several important roles to perform. The main function of trade unions in the past has been collective bargaining. This will continue to be central in the future, but under vastly different conditions. These include

- the recognition that in a high-discretion workplace, the individual becomes more important and individual differences in performance and rewards may be decisive in competition;
- a less adversarial relationship between labor and management in the pursuit of a common interest;
- the need for unions to possess greater knowledge of the management side of the picture and to assume more responsibility for the fate of the business;
- less rigidity with respect to work rules, and a much greater concern with productivity;
- a welcome rather than a rebuff of pluralistic forms of reward and pay for performance, with less sacredness attached to seniority;
- less emphasis on national bargaining and more on local, company-by-company agreements;
- greater responsibility for the education and training of members; and
- greater responsibility for shaping national policy, not as a special interest but as a representative of the overall health of the economy.

If there ever was a time for a fresh start in the trade union movement, it is today. If unions persist in supporting the old, discredited system of adversary relationships with employers, and most particularly in retaining the structured, autocratic organizations of the past, they are doomed to continued loss of membership. Unions will determine that they must be models of participation and of democracy in action if they are to play a central role in the new framework.

Jack Joyce, president of the International Union of Bricklayers and Allied Craftsmen, can serve as a model. In recent years he has inspired his archetypal trade union to become actively interested in the business side of bricklaying. The union has created marketing programs to encourage the use of brick in new applications and in architecture. It operates on the conviction that if it stimulates the industry to grow, more jobs and greater job security are the predictable results.

Education

The educational profession is making slow progress toward being included in the workplace consensus. The obstacles are formidable. Secondary schools find themselves at the center of competing demands that pull them in many directions at once. Every group in every community wants to use the schools to fulfill its own purposes and ideals, be they bilingual education, moral values, vocational training, athletic prowess, college preparation, back-to-basics, scientific literacy, cultural literacy, or better discipline. It is difficult for the schools to focus on a limited number of objectives and accomplish them well.

At the level of higher education, the private colleges find themselves in an increasingly severe financial squeeze. They too are pulled in many directions at once. But here the conflicting pressures come mainly from within. The subculture of higher education is a powerful one. There exists a strong tradition of isolation from the larger community, which many faculties uphold with pride. Scholars see it as a virtue that the campus can serve as a haven from the grime and sweat and materialistic strivings of the commercial world. At the very least, they feel ambivalent about responding once again to the call for "relevance" to the concerns of society as a whole. College faculties' greatest fear about more intimate involvement in the struggle for competitiveness is that it will deteriorate into vocationalism and that they will become an appendage to business in training students in industrial skills.

The dilemma for the country and for educators is acute. On the one hand, there is widespread recognition that education is a key to renewed competitiveness; the strategic role of education in Japan is a constant reminder of this truism. On the other hand, it is exceedingly difficult for educators at all levels to adapt to the new demands on them and also carry out the other tasks expected of them.

For better or worse, however, there is little choice for American teachers: the dilemma will ultimately be resolved in favor of greater involvement in the economic competition. If America does not succeed in improving its competitive position, education will be a big loser. Education consumes vast resources, and although Americans agree that they must sacrifice to give schools and colleges what they require (this conviction is one of America's oldest and most stable values), the resources have to be available, and Americans must be convinced that education has done its share in strengthening the country's competitive posture. The world of education, whatever its internal pressures and traditions, cannot remain aloof from or ineffectual in dealing with this issue.

Fortunately, there is growing clarity about what education needs to do. Clark Kerr's Commission on Global Education stresses the urgency of making today's students more "globally literate." (The commission's inquiries found among American students a "fundamental ignorance of how one nation's actions impact on [sic] the rest of us.")[11] The commission wishes to reorient secondary school curricula to impart to students a picture of the world as a closely linked community, "as if the world were round."[12] That is, the commission is seeking nothing less than a shift from America's traditional ethnocentrism to a global perspective — a shift of monumental proportions.

The Conference of the Nation's Governors has reached

similar conclusions. In their 1987 report, entitled "Jobs, Growth and Competitiveness," the governors stress the importance of education in preparing the nation to do a better job in the global marketplace. They place the blame for the country's mediocre performance on Americans' lack of understanding of the rest of the world and how to deal with it. The report concludes: "In the final analysis the best jobs, the largest markets and the greatest profits will flow to the workers and firms that understand the world around them. In most cases we do not." [13] To remedy the problem, the report stresses, we must improve the quality of education in our schools. It recommends that the schools restore geography as a distinct subject, improve instruction in foreign languages both at the elementary level and as a requirement for college admission, and do more to increase students' familiarity with modern technology.

Colleges and universities are also gaining a better understanding of what they must do if America is to become a more skillful player in the world economy. Fortunately for everyone, no one wants America's great system of higher education — one of the glories of our civilization — to degenerate into narrow vocationalism. The students do not want it: they want a college education that will permit them to fulfill their expressive values and not merely train them in making money (though the importance of making money cannot be minimized these days). The business community does not seek vocationalism either: in the fast-moving global economy, vocational skills quickly become obsolete. Besides, once jobholders move above the lowest ranks, business demands the skills of the generalist: mental flexibility, analytic skills, problem-solving ability, clarity in communicating, the ability to work well with others, a disciplined method for learning, and comfort in dealing with subjects that cut across the boundaries of specialists as well as of nations.

The colleges and universities have a special role to play in developing and commercializing technology. Increasingly, the sharp divisions among business, government, and universities are breaking down, and America's technological development is benefiting from the bonds being formed by industrial research and development, government-sponsored research, and university-based institutes.

Colleges must also contribute to the global "comfort level" of students. America's shift from ethnocentrism to a worldwide perspective will be accomplished mainly by the colleges and universities, which must prepare tomorrow's managers and professionals to be at home in the new global economy. Americans must learn more about the languages, cultures, and histories of other peoples, and more about how the commercial, cultural, and political systems of the world are linked.

The Community

We conclude with a note on local communities, whose role in the economic competition is indispensable but not obvious. Their task when it comes to schools is reasonably clear, but in America local communities do not effectively control any of the other major institutions — not large industries, which are national or international in scope; not the unions, most of which are also national; not even colleges and universities, many of which have national or statewide constituencies; and surely not federal or state government. Potentially, however, the influence of local communities extends far beyond the schools. As the logic of discretionary effort works itself out, they become an increasingly important part of the workplace consensus.

Consider, for example, the relationship of the local community to organized labor. The trade union movement reached the peak of its influence when the discretionary effort of the individual was at its lowest point. In assembly-line production, individuals had virtually no bargaining power in their own right. Individuals were interchangeable. The power resided in the collectivity, especially the national union; the local community was powerless. But decisions made at the national level failed to take local conditions into account, partly because the interests of the whole union were not always compatible with the interests of any one particular plant or community. In countries such as Sweden, where there is national bargaining across industries, the disparities between the interests of local communities and the national labor movement are even more glaring, with deleterious effects on competitiveness. This kind of conflict has also weakened the British economy.

In a more-for-more economy, decision making evolves from the national to the local level. This shift does not eliminate conflicts of interest: management and labor can be just as bitterly opposed in local communities as on the national level. But the adversarial relationship is not as rigidly institutionalized among people who have to live together in the same community and work together every day against a common competitor.

To the extent that labor and management are organized along national rather than local lines, an element of class conflict is present. Nothing can undermine America's efforts at improving competitiveness more quickly. If the effort to improve product quality, service, and cost effectiveness degenerates into a management interest, at odds with the interests of the individual jobholders, then the game is lost before it starts.

As we have suggested, the strategy of choice is not to weaken further the institutions of labor or management, but to organize everyone's loyalty and efforts at the local level rather than the national level. A more-for-more relationship in the workplace reduces the adversarial relations between workers and management. Under the old social contract, workers who won greater job security might have used it for featherbedding and other ways of giving less rather than more. Under a more-for-more contract, job security gives jobholders a positive incentive to take more initiative in working with new technology, reducing costs, and enhancing productivity.

In determining whether job security will really lead to greater commitment, the social environment of the local community is critical. When the Japanese open new plants in America, they carefully select communities that are inhospitable to national unions, so the Japanese owners gain flexibility in work rules and productivity improvements. The local community is a key factor not only in plant location but in the culture of the firm.

Most American firms do not have the option of starting over again without unions: they must make their deals with organized labor — or produce their products in other countries. A creative compromise is called for, under which organized labor will give greater autonomy to local unions and companies will pursue good-faith agreements in a nonadversarial spirit at the local level. The community can play a key role in shaping these arrangements.

If the economic competition is going to be won at the local level, the identities of the key players have to be found there. Each company, each plant, each division, each jobholder makes unique demands on a supportive environment. The local community is critical to supporting or failing to support environmental protection, child-care services, cultural and educational amenities, social support for those who need help, support to families, and so forth. Most individuals cannot hope to make a difference at the state or national level. But they can make an important contribution at the local level. Their communities are where they live and work, where they have their true identities.

Notes

Bibliography

Index

Notes

INTRODUCTION

1. For evidence of this drop in public support, see surveys conducted by CBS News/*New York Times*, April 15, 1986, through January 21, 1987.
2. Yankelovich, Skelly and White, Inc., for *Time*, 1982.
3. Roper Organization, for the American Enterprise Institute, November 1981.

CHAPTER 1

1. A. N. Whitehead, *Science and the Modern World* (Hammondsworth, England: Pelican Books, 1938), p. 22.

CHAPTER 2

1. George Kennan ("X"), "The Sources of Soviet Conduct," *Foreign Affairs* 25 (July 1947): 566–82, reprinted in George Kennan, *American Diplomacy, 1900–1950* (Chicago: University of Chicago Press, 1951), pp. 107–28; and Executive Secretary on United States Ob-

jectives and Programs for National Security, "NSC-68: A Report to the National Security Council," April 7, 1950, reprinted in *Naval War College Review* 27 (1975): 51–108.

2. John L. Gaddis, "The Rise, Fall and Future of Détente," *Foreign Affairs* (Winter 1983/84): 354–77.

3. Gallup Organization, Inc., 1949.

4. Speech given by Winston Churchill on March 5, 1946, at Westminster College, Fulton, Missouri. See Winston Churchill, "Sinews of Peace," *Vital Speeches* 12 (March 1946): 329–32. For a detailed discussion of the impact of this speech on U.S.-Soviet relations, see Fraser J. Harbutt, *The Iron Curtain: Churchill, America and the Origins of the Cold War* (Oxford: Oxford University Press, 1986).

5. John van Oudenaren, "Containment: Obsolete and Enduring Features," in *U.S.-Soviet Relations: The Next Phase,* ed. Arnold Horelick (Ithaca, N.Y.: Cornell University Press, 1986), p. 33.

6. Strobe Talbott, *Deadly Gambits: The Reagan Administration and the Stalemate in Nuclear Arms Control* (New York: Knopf, 1984), p. 206.

7. Harvard Nuclear Study Group, *Living with Nuclear Weapons* (Cambridge, Mass.: Harvard University Press, 1983), p. 87.

8. Ibid.

9. Ibid., p. 91.

10. Seweryn Bialer, "Lessons of History: Soviet-American Relations in the Post War Era," in *U.S.-Soviet Relations: The Next Phase,* ed. Arnold Horelick (Ithaca, N.Y.: Cornell University Press, 1986), p. 103. Richard Lowenthal also makes this point in "The Shattered Balance: Estimating the Dangers of War and Peace," *Encounter* 55 (November 1980): 12.

11. For a detailed discussion of U.S. and Soviet reactions to the events following détente, see Seweryn Bialer, *The Soviet Paradox: External Expansion, Internal Decline* (New York: Knopf, 1986), pp. 308–15.

12. Personal conversation with Marshall Shulman, 1985.

13. Paul Seabury, "Respecting Containment," in *Beyond Containment: Alternative American Policies Toward the Soviet Union,* ed. Aaron Wildavsky (San Francisco: Institute for Contemporary Studies Press, 1983), p. 54.

14. See Yankelovich, Skelly and White, Inc., for *Time*, 1980–1981.

15. Talbott, *Deadly Gambits*, p. 83.

16. Ibid., p. 348.

CHAPTER 3

1. William Schneider, " 'Rambo' and Reality: Having It Both Ways," in *Eagle Resurgent? The Reagan Era in American Foreign Policy*, eds. Kenneth A. Oye, Robert J. Lieber, and Donald Rothchild (Boston: Little, Brown, 1987), pp. 45–51.
2. Ibid.
3. Aaron Wildavsky, "Dilemmas of American Foreign Policy," in *Beyond Containment: Alternative American Policies Toward the Soviet Union*, ed. Aaron Wildavsky (San Francisco: Institute for Contemporary Studies Press, 1983), p. 17.
4. Roger Rosenblatt, "The Atomic Age," *Time* (July 29, 1985): 48–49.
5. Edward N. Luttwak, *The Pentagon and the Art of War* (New York: Simon & Schuster, 1984).
6. Comment made by Edward Luttwak in his speech to the Aspen Institute, June 8, 1985.
7. Public Agenda Foundation and Center for Foreign Policy Development at Brown University, "Voter Options on Nuclear Arms Policy: A Briefing Book for the 1984 Elections" (New York: Public Agenda Foundation, 1984). For a detailed breakdown of the survey questions by subgroups, see Public Agenda's "Voter Options on Nuclear Arms Policy: A Briefing Book for the 1984 Elections, Technical Appendix."
8. Ibid., p. 29; "Technical Appendix," p. 59.
9. Ibid.
10. Yankelovich, Skelly and White, Inc., for *Time*, December 1983.
11. See Roper Organization, February 1984; Gallup Organization, Inc., January 1985; and *Los Angeles Times*, January 1985, for evidence of this shift.

CHAPTER 4

1. Public Agenda Foundation and Center for Foreign Policy Development at Brown University, "Voter Options on Nuclear Arms Policy: A Briefing Book for the 1984 Elections" (New York: Public Agenda Foundation, 1984), p. 22.
2. Ibid., pp. 28–29.
3. Ibid.

4. Gallup Organization, Inc., March 1987.
5. Public Agenda Foundation and Center for Foreign Policy Development, "Voters Options," p. 24.
6. Ibid.
7. Ibid., p. 37.
8. Yankelovich, Skelly and White, Inc., for *Time*, December 1983.
9. Market Opinion Research, for the Americans Talk Security Project, January 1988. See also Roper Organization, June 1978, February 1980, and September 1984.

CHAPTER 5

1. Louis Harris and Associates, March 1983.
2. See Gallup Organization, Inc., October 1986, and Gallup Organization, Inc., for *Newsweek*, November 1985.
3. *Los Angeles Times*, November 1985.
4. Roper Organization, December 1982.
5. Public Agenda Foundation, May 1984.
6. Roper Organization, April 1983.
7. Public Agenda Foundation, May 1984.
8. CBS News/*New York Times*, October 1986.
9. Marttila & Kiley, Inc., for Women's Action for Nuclear Disarmament Education Fund, September 1985.

CHAPTER 6

1. Norman Podhoretz, "The Future Danger," *Commentary* (April 1981): 44.
2. See Robert McNamara, *Blundering into Disaster: Surviving the First Century of the Nuclear Age* (New York: Pantheon Books, 1986), Appendix II, p. 151.
3. Ibid., p. 8.

CHAPTER 7

1. Independent Commission on Disarmament and Security Issues, *Common Security: A Blueprint for Survival* (New York: Simon & Schuster, 1982), p. 139.

2. Ibid., p. xiii.

3. Comment made at the Dartmouth Conference, Moscow, USSR, January 1987.

4. Flora Lewis, "The Roots of Revolution," *New York Times Magazine,* November 11, 1984, pp. 70–83.

5. Ibid., p. 83.

CHAPTER 8

1. Robert S. McNamara and Hans A. Bethe, "Reducing the Risk of Nuclear War," *Atlantic Monthly* (July 1985): 51.

2. Commission on Integrated Long-Term Strategy, Department of Defense, "Discriminate Deterrence" (Washington, D.C.: U.S. Government Printing Office, 1988). For a brief summary of the report, see Bernard E. Trainor, "U.S. Urged to Cut Reliance on Nuclear Arms," *New York Times,* January 11, 1988, p. A7.

3. Personal correspondence, February 1987.

4. Randall Forsberg, "A Global Approach to Nonprovocative Defense," the first paper in the series "Alternative Defense Working Papers" (Brookline, Mass.: Institute for Defense and Disarmament Studies, forthcoming).

5. Frances Fukuyama, "U.S.-Soviet Interactions in the Third World," in *U.S.-Soviet Relations: The Next Phase,* ed. Arnold Horelick (Ithaca, N.Y.: Cornell University Press, 1986), pp. 198–224.

6. Aaron Wildavsky, "Dilemmas of American Foreign Policy," in *Beyond Containment: Alternative American Policies Toward the Soviet Union,* ed. Aaron Wildavsky (San Francisco: Institute for Contemporary Studies Press, 1983), pp. 17–18.

7. Comment made at the Dartmouth Conference on Political Relations, Washington, D.C., January 29–31, 1986.

8. One set of proposals to this end appears in William Ury and Richard Smoke, "Beyond the Hotline: Controlling a Nuclear Crisis," report to the U.S. Arms Control and Disarmament Agency (Cambridge, Mass.: Harvard Law School Nuclear Negotiation Project, 1984).

9. Harold H. Saunders, *The Other Walls: The Politics of the Arab-Israeli Peace Process* (Washington, D.C.: American Enterprise Institute for Public Policy Research, 1985).

10. Paul Kennedy, *The Rise and Fall of the Great Powers: Economic Change*

and Military Conflict from 1500 to 2000 (New York: Random House, 1987), p. xv–xxv.
11. The Daniel Yankelovich Group, Inc., for the Americans Talk Security Project, registered voters, March 1988.

CHAPTER 9

1. Ruben F. Mettler, paper presented to the Symposium on Economics and Technology, Stanford University, March 19, 1985.
2. Ruben F. Mettler, "America's Competitive Challenge," paper presented to the Conference Board, New York Marriott Marquis, April 23, 1986, p. 6.

CHAPTER 10

1. David Ricardo, *On Principles of Political Economy and Taxation* (Washington, D.C.: J. Milligan, 1919).
2. Bruce R. Scott, "National Strategy for Stronger U.S. Competitiveness," *Harvard Business Review* (March/April 1984): 86.
3. Lee Iacocca, "World Trade: What U.S. Firms Are Up Against," *Washington Post*, August 2, 1983, p. A17.
4. *Wall Street Journal*, February 25, 1985.

CHAPTER 11

1. See John A. Young, "Global Competition: The New Reality," vol. 1 (Washington, D.C.: U.S. Government Printing Office, 1985).
2. "Schultze Attacks Premise of New Industrial Policy," *Washington Post*, September 29, 1983, p. B2.
3. John L. Palmer and Isabel V. Sawhill, *The Reagan Record* (Cambridge Mass.: Ballinger Press, 1984), p. 20.
4. Coopers & Lybrand (U.S.A.) and Yankelovich, Skelly and White, Inc., "Business Planning in the Eighties: The New Competitiveness of American Corporations" (New York: Coopers & Lybrand, 1983).
5. Personal conversation, February 1987.

CHAPTER 12

1. Yankelovich, Skelly and White, Inc., "Meeting Japan's Challenge: The Need for Leadership" (Schaumburg, Ill.: Motorola, Inc., 1982), p. 4.
2. Business–Higher Education Forum, "America's Competitive Challenge: The Need for a National Response" (Washington, D.C.: Business–Higher Education Forum, 1983), p. i.
3. See *Los Angeles Times,* May 1984, October 1984, September 1985, February 1986; and CBS News/*New York Times,* January 1987.
4. Opinion Research Corporation, August 1987. See also Roper Organization, January 1987, for comparable findings.
5. Louis Harris and Associates, November 1985.
6. Louis Harris and Associates, for *Business Week,* June 1984.
7. *Los Angeles Times,* September 1985.
8. CBS News/*New York Times,* January 1986.
9. Louis Harris and Associates, for *Asahi Shimbun,* October 1986.
10. Yankelovich, Skelly and White, Inc., for *Time,* September 1985.
11. *Wall Street Journal,* October 1985.

CHAPTER 13

1. See Daniel Yankelovich and John Immerwahr, "Putting the Work Ethic to Work: A Public Agenda Report on Restoring America's Competitive Vitality" (New York: Public Agenda Foundation, 1983).

CHAPTER 14

1. For a more detailed discussion of early approaches to industrialized work, see Daniel T. Rogers, *The Work Ethic in Industrial America, 1850–1920* (Chicago: University of Chicago Press, 1974); W. J. Heisler and John W. Houch, *A Matter of Dignity* (South Bend, Ind.: University of Notre Dame Press, 1977); and Herbert Gutman, *Work, Culture and Society in Industrial America* (New York: Vintage Books, 1977).
2. Rogers, *The Work Ethic in Industrial America,* p. 55.
3. Daniel Yankelovich and John Immerwahr, "Putting the Work Ethic

to Work: A Public Agenda Report on Restoring America's Competitive Vitality" (New York: Public Agenda Foundation, 1983), p. 14.

4. For a detailed discussion as to how to introduce new technology in a way that stimulates jobholder acceptance and support, see Mary Komarnicki, Daniel Yankelovich, Sidney Harman, and John Immerwahr, "New Technology in the Workplace: A Quotebook of Opportunities and Options" (New York: Public Agenda Foundation, 1984).

5. Daniel Bell, *The Winding Passage* (New York: Basic Books, 1980).

6. Sar Levitan and Clifford Johnson, *Second Thoughts on Work* (Kalamazoo, Mich.: W. E. Upjohn Institute, 1982), p. 93.

7. Yankelovich and Immerwahr, "Putting the Work Ethic to Work," p. 17.

8. Ibid., p. 25.

9. Gallup Organization, Inc., for U.S. Chamber of Commerce, 1980. See Ronald Clarke and James Morris, "Worker Attitudes Toward Productivity" (Washington D.C.: U.S. Chamber of Commerce, 1980).

10. Yankelovich and Immerwahr, "Putting the Work Ethic to Work," p. 27.

11. Daniel Yankelovich, Hans Zetterberg, Burkhard Strumpel, and Michael Shanks, *The World at Work: An International Report on Jobs, Productivity, and Human Values* (New York: Octagon Books, 1985), p. 139.

12. Yankelovich and Immerwahr, "Putting the Work Ethic to Work," p. 27.

CHAPTER 15

1. Louis Harris and Associates, October 1983.

2. See "American Public Opinion and U.S. Foreign Policy 1987," ed. John E. Rielly (Chicago: Chicago Council on Foreign Relations, 1987), p. 37.

3. Roper Organization, August 1984.

4. Louis Harris and Associates, for Southern New England Telephone, September 1983.

5. Analysis Group, January 1985.

6. *Los Angeles Times,* January 1985.

7. See Morris E. Morkre and David G. Tarr, "Effects of Restrictions

on United States Imports," a Bureau of Economics Staff report to the Federal Trade Commission (Washington, D.C.: U.S. Government Printing Office, 1980); David G. Tarr and Morris E. Morkre, "Aggregate Costs to the United States of Tariffs and Quotas on Imports," a Bureau of Economics Staff report to the Federal Trade Commission (Washington, D.C.: U.S. Government Printing Office, 1984); Congress of the United States, Congressional Budget Office, "Dislocated Workers: Issues and Federal Options" (Washington, D.C.: U.S. Government Printing Office, 1982); and Congress of the United States, Office of Technological Assessment, "Technology and Structural Unemployment: Re-employing Displaced Adults" (Washington, D.C.: U.S. Government Printing Office, 1986).

CHAPTER 16

1. American Council of Life Insurance and Health Insurance Association of America, "The Baby Boom Generation" (Washington, D.C.: American Council of Life Insurance and Health Insurance Association of America, 1983), p. 9.
2. U.S. Bureau of Labor Statistics, *Employment and Earnings*. Cited in U.S. Bureau of the Census, *Statistical Abstracts of the United States: 1987* (Washington, D.C.: U.S. Government Printing Office, 1986), p. 376.
3. American Council of Life Insurance and Health Insurance Association of America, "The Baby Boom Generation," p. 17.
4. Ibid., p. 14.
5. For a detailed discussion of "expressive values," see Daniel Yankelovich, Hans Zetterberg, Burkhard Strumpel, and Michael Shanks, *The World at Work: An International Report on Jobs, Productivity, and Human Values* (New York: Octagon Books, 1985), pp. 33–39.
6. Yankelovich, Skelly and White, Inc., for *Time*, December 1984.
7. Roper Organization, December 1984.
8. Daniel Yankelovich and John Immerwahr, "Putting the Work Ethic to Work: A Public Agenda Report on Restoring America's Competitive Vitality" (New York: Public Agenda Foundation, 1983), p. 21.
9. Jeylan Mortimer, Michael Finch, and Geoffrey Maruyama, "Work and Job Satisfaction," paper presented at the annual meeting of the American Association for the Advancement of Science, Los Angeles, May 1985.

10. Quoted in Bruce W. Most, "Jack MacAllister: Hands-Off Management," *American Way* (American Airlines, October 29–November 11, 1985): 44.
11. See "National Report Shows Why Johnny Can't Read the Globe: Study Commission Warns America's Children Are Globally Illiterate," May 12, 1987, press release for the Study Commission on Global Education, "The United States Prepares for Its Future: Global Perspectives in Education" (New York: Global Perspectives, Inc., 1987), p. 1.
12. Ibid., p. 2.
13. William K. Stevens, "Governors Assert Key to Prosperity in Global View: Their Report Puts Emphasis on Broad Steps to Bolster U.S. Competitiveness," *New York Times*, July 26, 1987, p. 22.

Bibliography

American Council of Life Insurance and the Health Insurance Association of America. "The Baby Boom Generation." Washington, D.C.: American Council of Life Insurance and the Health Insurance Association of America, 1983.

Bell, Daniel. *The Winding Passage*. New York: Basic, 1980.

Bialer, Seweryn. "Lessons of History: Soviet-American Relations in the Post War Era." In *U.S.-Soviet Relations: The Next Phase*. Ed. Arnold Horelick. Ithaca, N.Y.: Cornell University Press, 1986.

Bialer, Seweryn. *The Soviet Paradox: External Expansion, Internal Decline*. New York: Knopf, 1986.

Business—Higher Education Forum. "America's Competitive Challenge: The Need for a National Response." Washington, D.C.: Business—Higher Education Forum, April 1983.

Churchill, Winston. "Sinews of Peace." *Vital Speeches* 12 (March 1946): 329–32.

Clarke, Ronald, and James Morris. "Worker Attitudes Toward Productivity." Washington, D.C.: U.S. Chamber of Commerce, 1980.

Commission on Integrated Long-Term Strategy. U.S. Department of Defense. "Discriminate Deterrence." Washington, D.C.: U.S. Government Printing Office, 1988.

Congress of the United States. Congressional Budget Office. "Dislocated Workers: Issues and Federal Options." Washington, D.C.: U.S. Government Printing Office, 1982.

Congress of the United States. Office of Technological Assessment. "Technology and Structural Unemployment: Re-employing Displaced Adults." Washington, D.C.: U.S. Government Printing Office, 1986.

Coopers & Lybrand (U.S.A.) and Yankelovich, Skelly and White, Inc. "Business Planning in the Eighties: The New Competitiveness of American Corporations." New York: Coopers & Lybrand (U.S.A.), 1983.

Executive Secretary on United States Objectives and Programs for National Security. "NSC-68: A Report to the National Security Council," April 7, 1950. Reprinted in *Naval War College Review* 27 (1975): 51–108.

Forsberg, Randall. "A Global Approach to Nonprovocative Defense." The first paper in the series "Alternative Defense Working Papers." Brookline, Mass.: Institute for Defense and Disarmament Studies, forthcoming.

Fukuyama, Francis. "U.S.-Soviet Interactions in the Third World." In *U.S.-Soviet Relations: The Next Phase*. Ed. Arnold Horelick. Ithaca, N.Y.: Cornell University Press, 1986.

Gaddis, John L. "The Rise, Fall and Future of Détente." *Foreign Affairs* (Winter 1983/84): 354–77.

Gutman, Herbert. *Work, Culture and Society in Industrial America*. New York: Vintage, 1977.

Harbutt, Fraser J. *The Iron Curtain: Churchill, America and the Origins of the Cold War*. Oxford: Oxford University Press, 1986.

Harvard Nuclear Study Group. *Living with Nuclear Weapons*. New York: Bantam, 1983.

Heisler, W. J., and John W. Houch. *A Matter of Dignity*. South Bend., Ind.: University of Notre Dame Press, 1977.

Iacocca, Lee. "World Trade: What U.S. Firms Are Up Against." *Washington Post,* August 2, 1983.

Independent Commission on Disarmament and Security Issues. *Common Security: A Blueprint for Survival*. New York: Simon & Schuster, 1982.

Kennan, George. *American Diplomacy, 1900–1950*. Chicago: University of Chicago Press, 1951.

Kennan, George ("X"). "The Sources of Soviet Conduct." *Foreign Affairs* 25 (July 1947): 566–82.

Kennedy, Paul. *The Rise and Fall of the Great Powers: Economic Change and Military Conflict from 1500 to 2000.* New York: Random House, 1987.

Komarnicki, Mary, Daniel Yankelovich, Sidney Harman, and John Immerwahr. "New Technology in the Workplace: A Quotebook of Opportunities and Options." New York: The Public Agenda Foundation, 1984.

Levitan, Sar, and Clifford Johnson. *Second Thoughts on Work.* Kalamazoo, Mich.: W. E. Upjohn Institute, 1982.

Lewis, Flora. "The Roots of Revolution." *New York Times Magazine* (November 11, 1984): 70–83.

Lowenthal, Richard. "The Shattered Balance: Estimating the Dangers of War and Peace." *Encounter* 55 (November 1980): 9–14.

Luttwak, Edward N. *The Pentagon and the Art of War.* New York: Simon & Schuster, 1984.

McNamara, Robert S. *Blundering into Disaster: Surviving the First Century of the Nuclear Age.* New York: Pantheon, 1986.

McNamara, Robert S., and Hans A. Bethe. "Reducing the Risk of Nuclear War." *Atlantic Monthly* (July 1985): 43–51.

Mettler, Ruben F. "America's Competitive Challenge." Paper presented to the Conference Board, New York Marriott Marquis, April 23, 1986.

Mettler, Ruben F. Paper presented to the Symposium on Economics and Technology, Stanford University, March 18, 1985.

Morkre, Morris E., and David G. Tarr. "Effects of Restrictions on United States Imports." A Bureau of Economics Staff report to the Federal Trade Commission. Washington, D.C.: U.S. Government Printing Office, 1980.

Mortimer, Jeylan, Michael Finch, and Geoffrey Maruyama. "Work and Job Satisfaction." Paper presented at the annual meeting of the American Association for the Advancement of Science, Los Angeles, May 1985.

Most, Bruce W. "Jack MacAllister: Hands-Off Management." *American Way* (American Airlines; October 29–November 11, 1985): 44–49.

Palmer, John L., and Isabel V. Sawhill. *The Reagan Record.* Cambridge, Mass.: Ballinger, 1984.

Podhoretz, Norman. "The Future Danger." *Commentary* (April 1981): 29–47.

Public Agenda Foundation and the Center for Foreign Policy Development at Brown University. "Voter Options on Nuclear Arms

Policy: A Briefing Book for the 1984 Elections." New York: The Public Agenda Foundation, 1984.

Public Agenda Foundation and the Center for Foreign Policy Development at Brown University. "Voter Options on Nuclear Arms Policy: A Briefing Book for the 1984 Elections, Technical Appendix." New York: The Public Agenda Foundation, 1984.

Ricardo, David. *On Principles of Political Economy and Taxation.* Washington, D.C.: J. Milligan, 1919.

Rielly, John E., ed. "American Public Opinion and U.S. Foreign Policy 1987." Chicago: The Chicago Council on Foreign Relations, 1987.

Rogers, Daniel T. *The Work Ethic in Industrial America, 1850–1920.* Chicago: University of Chicago Press, 1974.

Rosenblatt, Roger. "The Atomic Age." *Time* (July 29, 1985): 32–59.

Saunders, Harold H. *The Other Walls: The Politics of the Arab-Israeli Peace Process.* Washington, D.C.: American Enterprise Institute for Public Policy Research, 1985.

Schneider, William. " 'Rambo' and Reality: Having It Both Ways." In *Eagle Resurgent? The Reagan Era in American Foreign Policy.* Eds. Kenneth A. Oye, Robert J. Lieber, and Donald Rothchild. Boston: Little, Brown, 1987.

Scott, Bruce R. "National Strategy for Stronger U.S. Competitiveness." *Harvard Business Review* 62 (March/April 1984): 77–91.

Seabury, Paul. "Respecting Containment." In *Beyond Containment: Alternative American Policies Toward the Soviet Union.* Ed. Aaron Wildavsky. San Francisco: Institute for Contemporary Studies Press, 1983.

Stevens, William K. "Governors Assert Key to Prosperity Is in Global View: Their Report Puts Emphasis on Broad Steps to Bolster U.S. Competitiveness." *New York Times,* July 26, 1987.

Study Commission on Global Education. "The United States Prepares for Its Future: Global Perspectives in Education." New York: Global Perspectives, Inc., 1987.

Talbott, Strobe. *Deadly Gambits: The Reagan Administration and the Stalemate in Nuclear Arms Control.* New York: Knopf, 1984.

Tarr, David G., and Morris E. Morkre. "Aggregate Costs to the United States of Tariffs and Quotas on Imports." A Bureau of Economics Staff report to the Federal Trade Commission. Washington, D.C.: U.S. Government Printing Office, 1984.

Trainor, Bernard E. "U.S. Urged to Cut Reliance on Nuclear Arms." *New York Times,* January 11, 1988, p. A7.

Ury, William, and Richard Smoke. "Beyond the Hotline: Controlling a Nuclear Crisis." A Report to the U.S. Arms Control and Disarmament Agency. Cambridge, Mass: Harvard Law School Nuclear Negotiation Project, 1984.

U.S. Bureau of the Census. *Statistical Abstracts of the United States: 1987.* Washington, D.C.: U.S. Government Printing Office, 1986.

Van Oudenaren, John. "Containment: Obsolete and Enduring Features." In *U.S.-Soviet Relations: The Next Phase.* Ed. Arnold Horelick. Ithaca, N.Y.: Cornell University Press, 1986.

Whitehead, Alfred North. *Science and the Modern World.* Harmondsworth, England: Pelican, 1938.

Wildavsky, Aaron. "Dilemmas of American Foreign Policy." In *Beyond Containment: Alternative American Policies Toward the Soviet Union.* Ed. Aaron Wildavsky. San Francisco: Institute for Contemporary Studies Press, 1983.

Yankelovich, Daniel, and John Immerwahr. "Putting the Work Ethic to Work: A Public Agenda Report on Restoring America's Competitive Vitality." New York: The Public Agenda Foundation, 1983.

Yankelovich, Skelly and White, Inc. "Meeting Japan's Challenge: The Need for Leadership." A study of American leaders' opinions on the Japanese challenge to American industry conducted for Motorola, Inc. Schaumburg, Ill.: Motorola, Inc., 1982.

Yankelovich, Daniel, Hans Zetterberg, Burkhard Strumpel, and Michael Shanks. *The World at Work: An International Report on Jobs, Productivity, and Human Values.* New York: Octagon, 1985.

Young, John A. "Global Competition: The New Reality." Vol. 1. Washington, D.C.: U.S. Government Printing Office, 1985.

Index